PC HARDWARE

BUYER'S GUIDE

CHOOSING THE PERFECT COMPONENTS

PC HARDWARE
BUYER'S GUIDE

CHOOSING THE PERFECT COMPONENTS

Robert Bruce Thompson & Barbara Fritchman Thompson

O'REILLY®

Beijing • Cambridge • Farnham • Köln • Paris • Sebastopol • Taipei • Tokyo

PC Hardware Buyer's Guide
Choosing the Perfect Components
by Robert Bruce Thompson and Barbara Fritchman Thompson

Printed in the United States of America.

Published by O'Reilly Media, Inc., 1005 Gravenstein Highway North, Sebastopol, CA 95472.

O'Reilly books may be purchased for educational, business, or sales promotional use. Online editions are also available for most titles (*safari.oreilly.com*). For more information, contact our corporate/institutional sales department: 800-998-9938 or *corporate@oreilly.com*.

Editor: Brian Jepson
Production Editor: Darren Kelly
Cover Designer: Marcia Friedman
Interior Designer: Marcia Friedman

Print History: February 2005: First Edition.

RepKover. This book uses RepKover™, a durable and flexible lay-flat binding.

0-596-00938-0
[M]

To Mark Brokering,
who came up with the idea and kept the ball rolling.

Table of Contents

Preface

Things change constantly in the PC component market. New products are introduced every day, and old ones disappear. Everything is in a constant state of flux. Keeping up with the current state of the PC component market is a full-time job. And it's our job to make sense of it all for you. That's what this book is for.

When we wrote *Building the Perfect PC* (O'Reilly), we took pains to ensure the book was completely current when it went to the printer. Even so, some of the information was outdated even before the book arrived in the bookstores. For example, we recommended Hitachi flat-panel displays only to learn literally days after our final chance to update the manuscript that Hitachi was departing the flat-panel display market. Oh, well.

So, one reason we wrote this book was to provide updated component recommendations. There was an even more important reason, though. Like most books, *Building the Perfect PC* had what authors and publishers call a "page-count budget." A longer book costs more to produce, and must sell for a higher price. In order to meet the target price, we had to stay within the page count budget. Doing that was painful.

Our first draft of the "Choosing and Buying Components" chapter for *Building the Perfect PC* was nearly 45,000 words. That would have translated to about 100 book pages, which is to say nearly a third of the entire book. As important as that material was, we simply couldn't afford to devote that many pages to it. Using that chapter at its original length would have meant dropping at least one, and perhaps two, of the five project system chapters, and we didn't want to do that. So we spent two weeks cutting the chapter to its eventual final length of about 18,000 words or 40 book pages. We think we did a pretty good job slimming the chapter down, too, but a lot of useful information ended up on the cutting room floor.

After discussing it with our editors, we decided the best solution was to convert that original monster chapter into a new Pocket Guide book to choosing and buying PC components. That gave us the best of all worlds. We would have the space to present the material at its original full length. We would have the chance to update the material to cover components and technologies that were unavailable when we wrote *Building the Perfect PC*. And, not least, we'd have the opportunity to package the information in a small, portable format.

Don't underestimate the importance of that last item, particularly if you buy some or all your components locally, as most PC builders do. Certainly, you can prepare a component list at home before you go shopping. But what if one (or several) of the components you chose isn't available?

We've been faced with that ourselves. We decided to buy a monitor one day, and we knew exactly which make and model we wanted. We drove to the big-box store, whose web site listed the monitor as in stock. It wasn't. So, there we stood, in an aisle with twenty different monitors, none of which were the one we wanted. If we'd had this book, we'd have been able to choose a good alternative with confidence.

Take this book with you when you buy components, and you won't have to make a decision with inadequate information.

How to Use the Quick Reference

The Quick Reference packs a great deal of information into a small space. We had to make use of a key and other shortcuts to make everything fit, so the Quick Reference may appear cryptic at first glance. Spend a few minutes reading this section, though, and all will become clear.

Here is a list of the icons used, with an explanation of what each icon means.

- 🌐 – suitable for any PC
- ✂ – economy PC or component
- 🏭 – business PC or component
- 🚴 – mainstream PC or component
- 🚗 – performance PC or component
- ♜ – gaming PC or component
- ⊙ – small form factor PC or component
- 🔈 – quiet PC or component
- 🐧 – Linux PC or component
- ✸ – other/special consideration

Our primary recommendations are **bolded** and we use filled bullets to separate groups by degree of preference. For example

a • b, c, or d • e

indicates that "a" is our primary recommendation, "b, c, or d" lists our three secondary recommendations (any of which is equally acceptable), and "e" is our tertiary recommendation, which is less desirable than the primary or secondary recommendations, but still acceptable.

We use dollar symbols to indicate the approximate price range of components and systems, as follows:

$ – budget system or component
$$ – mainstream system or component
$$$ – premium system or component
$$$$ – ultra-premium system or component

Note that the absolute prices within these categories differ according to the type of component. For example, a ($) CD burner might cost $30, a ($) processor or video adapter $75, and a ($) 19" flat-panel display $400, but each is a budget component within the range of prices typical for similar components.

In general, a ($) component is one that is inferior to its more costly counterparts in functionality, performance, and/or reliability, but is sufficiently less expensive to make it a reasonable choice if you are building a system on a tight budget. Mass-market and consumer-grade systems generally use ($) components (or worse). Mainstream ($$) components are the best choice for most systems. They cost a bit more than ($) components, but the additional cost is small relative to the increased functionality, performance, and reliability. Premium ($$$) components are on the wrong side of the price/performance curve. They are better than ($$) components, certainly, but their additional cost is often too high to justify. Ultra-premium ($$$$) components are a step farther out along the bad side of the price/performance curve.

Dissecting a cheap PC

So, just how bad are the components used in mass-market PCs? We decided to find out, so we sent our Mystery Shopper off to make the rounds of the big-box stores, looking for a midrange consumer-grade system.

When our Mystery Shopper returned to the Bat Cave, Robert and Barbara donned their scrubs and set to work, disassembling the patient and analyzing each component. What did they find? A cheap motherboard? Slow memory? A cheap, unstable power supply? Stay tuned to find out...

We didn't have room to include the postmortem report here, but you can read it online at *http://www.windowsdevcenter/buildPC.html.*

Warning: This report includes graphic, full-color images.

So why do premium and ultra-premium components even exist? Because some people want the best and are willing to pay for it. For example, although we list several usable ($) 2.0 speaker sets for $20 or so, we also list ($$) sets at twice that price. The $20 budget sets are a good value for the money, but most people perceive a noticeable improvement in sound quality with the ($$) mainstream sets. The next step up, the ($$$) premium M-Audio sets are $120 components. Do they sound three times as good as the $40 mainstream sets? No, but they do sound better. And the ultra-premium Swans 2.0 set costs $180 or so. If you think that's outrageous for a 2.0 speaker set, you're not alone. We completely agree, but try telling an audiophile that. They swear there's a difference, and that it's worth the extra cost to them. We believe them, too. As the Romans said, *de gustibus non est disputandum* (roughly translated, "there is no arguing about taste").

Of course, the specific brand and model recommendations in this book may be outdated as quickly as those in *Building the Perfect PC*, although the other information we provide has a much longer shelf life. To extend the useful life of this book, we plan to produce updated Quick Reference data, which you can download from our web site. We distribute the updated Quick Reference as a .PDF file, formatted so you can cut it out and tape it inside the cover. To download the most recent version of the Quick Reference, point your browser to *http://www.hardwareguys.com/quickref/quickref.html.* At the login prompt, enter the following account information:

Username: quickref

Password: quickref

Acknowledgments

In addition to the O'Reilly production staff, who are listed individually in the Colophon, we want to thank our "kitchen cabinet"—Brian Bilbrey, Roland Dobbins, Greg Lincoln, Francisco García Maceda, Ron Morse, and Jerry Pournelle—a group of friends and colleagues who read the early drafts of this material and made numerous helpful comments, corrections, and suggestions.

We also want to thank our contacts at the hardware companies, who provided technical help, evaluation units, and other assistance. There are far too many to list individually, but they know who they are. We also want to thank the readers of our websites and messageboards, many of whom have taken the time to offer useful suggestions for improvements to the book. Thanks, folks. We couldn't have done it without you.

Finally, we want to thank our O'Reilly editors, Brian Jepson and Mark Brokering, both of whom contributed numerous useful comments and suggestions.

We'd Like to Hear from You

We have tested and verified the information in this book to the best of our ability, but we don't doubt that some errors have crept in and remained hidden despite our best efforts, and those of our editors and technical reviewers, to find and eradicate them. Those errors are ours alone. If you find an error or have other comments about the book, you can contact the publisher or the authors.

How to Contact O'Reilly

Please address comments and questions concerning this book to the publisher:

O'Reilly Media, Inc.
1005 Gravenstein Highway North
Sebastopol, CA 95472
800-998-9938 (in the United States or Canada)
707-829-0515 (international or local)
707-829-0104 (fax)

You can also send us email. For comments on the book, send email to *bookquestions@oreilly.com*.

The web site for *PC Hardware Buyer's Guide* lists examples, errata, and plans for future editions. You can find this page at: *http://www.oreilly.com/catalog/pccbg*.

For more information about this book and others, see the O'Reilly web site: *http://www.oreilly.com*.

How to Contact the Authors

To contact one of the authors directly, send mail to: *barbara@hardwareguys.com* or *robert@hardwareguys.com*.

We read all mail we receive from readers, but we cannot respond individually. If we did, we'd have no time to do anything else. But we do like to hear from you.

There is also a web site for the book, which includes updated hardware recommendations, buying guides, and articles, as well as errata, archived older material, and so on: *http://www.hardwareguys.com*.

We also maintain a messageboard, where you can read and post messages about PC hardware topics. You can read messages as a guest, but if you want to post messages you must register as a member of the messageboard. We keep registration information confidential, and you can choose to have your mail address hidden on any messages you post. Check it out at: *http://forums.hardwareguys.com/*

We each maintain a personal journal page, updated daily, which frequently includes references to new PC hardware we're working with, problems we've discovered, and other things we think are interesting. You can view these journal pages at:

Barbara: *http://www.fritchman.com/diaries/thisweek.html*

Robert: *http://www.ttgnet.com/thisweek.html*

Thank You

Thank you for buying the *PC Hardware Buyer's Guide*. We hope you enjoy reading it as much as we enjoyed writing it.

1

Choosing Components

The biggest advantage of building your own PC is that you can choose which components to use. If you buy a cookie-cutter system from Dell or HP, most of the decisions are made for you. You can specify a larger hard drive, more memory, or a different monitor, but the range of options is quite limited. Want a better power supply, a quieter CPU cooler, and a motherboard with built-in Gigabit Ethernet, FireWire, and RAID 0+1 support? Tough luck. Those options aren't on the table.

When you build from scratch, you get to choose every component that goes into your system. You can spend a bit more here and a bit less there to get exactly the features and functions you want at the best price. It's therefore worth devoting some time and effort to component selection, but there are so many competing products available that it's difficult to separate the marketing hype from reality.

On your own, you might find yourself struggling to answer questions like, "Should I buy a Seagate hard drive or a Western Digital?" (hint: Seagate) or "Does Sony or HP make the best DVD writers?" (hint: neither; go with a Plextor). We've done all that research for you, and the following sections distill what we've learned in testing and using hundreds of products over many years.

We recommend products by brand name, and we don't doubt that some people will take issue with some of our recommendations. We don't claim that the products we recommend are "best" in any absolute sense, because we haven't tested every product on the market and because "best" is inherently subjective. What's "best" for us may be just "very good" from your point of view, but it almost certainly won't be "awful."

So, keeping all of that in mind, the following sections describe the products we recommend.

Details, details...

For more detailed selection criteria and in-depth explanations of technical issues related to choosing components, see the current edition of *PC Hardware in a Nutshell* (O'Reilly).

Case

The case (or chassis) is the foundation of any system. Its obvious purpose is to support the power supply, motherboard, drives, and other components. Its less-obvious purposes are to contain the radio-frequency interference produced by internal components, to ensure proper system cooling, and to subdue the noise produced by the power supply, drives, fans, and other components with moving parts.

A good case performs all of these tasks well, and is a joy to work with. It is strongly built and rigid. Adding or removing components is quick and easy. All the holes line up. There are no sharp edges or burrs. A bad case is painful to work with, sometimes literally. It may have numerous exposed razor-sharp edges and burrs that cut you even if you're careful. It is cheaply constructed of flimsy material that flexes excessively. Tolerances are very loose, sometimes so much so that you have to bend sheet metal to get a component to fit, if that is even possible. Using a cheap case is a sure way to make your system building experience miserable. Figure 1-1 shows the interior of the Antec Sonata, our favorite general-purpose case.

FIGURE 1-1. **The Antec Sonata case**

Use the following guidelines when choosing a case:

Choose the appropriate size

Mainstream PC cases are available in sizes from full-tower down to about the size of a VCR. SFF (Small Form Factor) cases are about the size and shape of a large shoe box. Choose the proper size case for your system, taking into account the original configuration and possible future expansion. For most general-purpose systems, the best compromise between size and capacity is a mini- or mid-tower case like the Antec Sonata. Such cases have plenty of expansion room—some can hold as many as nine drives—but are small enough to fit most workspaces. For a small PC, the best choice is usually a microATX case such as the Antec Aria that uses industry-standard motherboards and other components.

What the Heck is BTX?

In mid-2004, Intel began shipping products based on their new ***Balanced Technology Extended*** (***BTX***) form factor, which will eventually replace ATX and its variants. BTX and its smaller variants, microBTX and picoBTX, are primarily a response to cooling problems and other inadequacies in the ATX specification that became evident as the power consumption and heat production of modern processors has continued to increase.

Bizarrely, the BTX specification denominates dimensions in millimeters, although those dimensions were obviously converted from inches. For example, all BTX motherboards, including the smaller BTX variants, must be 266.70 mm deep. If you do the math, you'll find that 266.70 mm converts to 10.50". Similarly, the width of a BTX motherboard must be 325.12 mm (12.80"); of a microBTX motherboard, 264.16 mm (10.40"); and of a picoBTX motherboard, 203.20 mm (8.00").

Although BTX motherboard sizes differ little from ATX and its variants, BTX specifies many changes in component layout and orientation, cooling, physical mounting, and so on. BTX motherboards and cases are of similar size and appearance to their ATX analogs, but are physically incompatible with those earlier components.

continued

In practical terms, the arrival of BTX is likely to have little short-term effect on system builders and upgraders. Migration to BTX will not occur overnight—although Intel would like it to—but will take place gradually over a period of months and years. ATX motherboards, cases, power supplies, and other components will remain available for years to come. During the early part of this migration, BTX components will be scarce and will likely sell at a premium. By late 2005 and into 2006, BTX components will become increasingly mainstream, with ATX gradually becoming relegated to upgrade-only status.

In short, you needn't be concerned about building an ATX-based system now, because upgrade components are likely to remain available for the usable life of the system. In fact, we are likely to continue recommending ATX in preference to BTX well into 2005, based on the lower cost and wider component availability of ATX components.

For more information about BTX, see the ***Balanced Technology Extended (BTX) Interface Specification Version 1.0*** at *http://www.formfactors.org.*

Small versus too small

microATX, SFF, and other "small" cases impose severe restrictions on expansion. They provide few drive bays and expansion slots, and may accept only half-height expansion cards. Cooling may be problematic with such cases because the volume is small and they have only one or two small fans. Use a small case only if size is a very important consideration.

Plan for expansion

For a general-purpose PC, choose a case that leaves at least one drive bay—ideally a 5.25" external bay—free for later expansion. At some point during the life of the system, you may want to install a second (or third) hard drive, a DVD writer, or some other component that requires a free drive bay. A mini/mid-tower case with at least two external 5.25" bays, one or two external 3.5" bays, and two or three internal 3.5" bays is usually the best choice. If in doubt, buy the next size up.

Avoid cheap cases

It's always tempting to save money, but cases are one place where it's easy to spend too little. The cheapest cases ($30 or $40 with power supply) are often unusable because of misaligned holes and so on. Even midrange "name brand" cases may have razor-sharp edges and burrs, which can cut you and short out wires. Expect to pay at least $40 (without power supply) for a decent mini or mid-tower case, and $60 for a full tower. Paying one and a half times as much usually gets you a much better case.

Buy case and power supply separately, if necessary

Cheap and midrange cases usually include a "throw away" power supply that's undersized and of poor quality. If you have such a case, do yourself a favor: discard the bundled power supply and install one of the power supplies we recommend. At best, cheap power supplies cause reliability problems. At worst, a cheap power supply may fail catastrophically, taking the motherboard and other system components with it. Better cases may be sold with or without a power supply. If the standard power supply is appropriate, you may save a few bucks by buying the bundle. Otherwise, buy only the case and install a high-quality power supply sized appropriately for your needs. Standard ATX power supplies fit standard ATX cases interchangeably, so compatibility is not an issue.

Get a case with supplemental cooling fans (or space to add them)

Heat is the enemy of processors, memory, drives, and other system components. Cooler components last longer and run more reliably. A processor run at 50° C (122° F), for example, may be twice as likely to fail as one run at 40° C (104° F), but half as likely as one run at 60° C (140° F). The best way to minimize temperature inside the case is to move a lot of air through it. Although the power supply fan and processor fan may provide adequate cooling on lightly loaded systems, adding supplemental fans can reduce ambient case temperature by 20° C (36° F) or more on more heavily loaded systems.

Many cases can be ordered with optional supplemental fans. If the case you choose offers optional fans, order them. Otherwise, add the fans yourself. You can purchase supplemental fans for a few dollars from local computer stores and mail-order suppliers. They are available in various standard sizes from 60 mm to 120 mm, so make sure to purchase the correct size. Note that many cases that accept multiple fans use different sizes in different locations.

Why large = quiet

If noise level is important to you, choose a case that accepts large fans. A large fan, such as a 120 mm unit, can run slower while moving the same amount of air as a faster-spinning smaller fan. All other things being equal, a fast-spinning fan makes more noise and at more intrusive frequencies than a slower fan. The amount of air a

fan moves is proportional to the surface area of its blades, which in turn is roughly proportional to the square of its radius. For example, a 120 mm fan running at a given speed moves four times as much air as a similar 60 mm fan. In fact, the 120 mm fan has an even larger advantage, because its hub occupies proportionately less of the available surface area than does the hub on a 60 mm fan. Also note that there are significant differences in noise level among different fans of the same size. Generally, ball-bearing fans are noisier but more reliable than fans that use sleeve or needle bearings.

Consider accessibility
: If you frequently add and remove components, consider purchasing a tool-free case with accessibility features such as snap-off side panels and a removable motherboard tray and drive bays. If you don't open your case from one month to the next, you may be better served by a case with fewer accessibility features, which is likely to be less expensive for equivalent quality and rigidity.

Consider shipping costs
: When you compare case prices, remember that shipping an individual case is expensive. Mail order companies often charge $20 to $40 or more to ship a case, depending on its size and weight. Big-box stores receive shipments on pallets via tractor trailers, so their cost to ship each individual case is very small. That is often reflected in their prices. It often costs less to buy a case locally, even after paying sales tax, than it does to order the same case from a mail-order vendor and pay shipping.

What to buy

Over the years we've used scores of different cases from a dozen or more makers. For the last several years, we've used and recommended Antec cases almost exclusively. Antec (*http://www.antec-inc.com*) offers a broad range of cases in sizes from microATX to full tower and server models. They have several product lines, including the value-priced Solution Series, the portable LANBOY Series, the mainstream Performance Series, and the specialized Lifestyle Series. Every Antec case we have used has been well designed, solidly constructed, and finely finished. Less expensive Antec cases include a decent midrange SmartPower power supply. Some premium Antec case models include their superb TruePower Series power supplies. Antec cases enjoy wide retail distribution, and are readily available at big-box stores and other local retailers.

Here are the cases we recommend for specific purposes:

Economy System

If you're putting together a system on a tight budget, use the beige **Antec SLK1650** Mini Tower case or the black **Antec SLK1650B** model. Both are suitable for AMD or Intel systems, including the hot-running Prescott-core Pentium 4, and both include a decent 350W SmartPower power supply. If you need a larger case, choose the **Antec SLK2650BQE** Mid Tower or the **Antec SLK3700BQE** Super Mid Tower. Both BQE (Black Quiet Edition) models include the 350W SmartPower power supply, and both are designed for quiet operation.

Business or Mainstream System

For a business or a mainstream system, choose the **Antec Sonata**. The Sonata is the most flexible case we've used and is appropriate for nearly any purpose. The Sonata is well-engineered, has excellent build quality, is very quiet, provides plenty of expansion room, and includes the excellent TruePower 380W power supply. We don't know of a better general-purpose case. If the Sonata is a bit much for your budget, the Antec SLK2650BQE or SLK3700BQE is a good alternative.

Performance or Gaming System

The aluminum Super Mid Tower **Antec P-160** is our choice for a performance system. The P-160 is light, has top-notch build quality, and provides excellent cooling. For a portable performance or gaming system, choose the **Antec Super LANBOY**. The P-160 and Super LANBOY come without a power supply, so you can choose the most appropriate power supply for your configuration. For a performance or gaming system on a tighter budget, choose the **Antec Sonata** if its 380W power supply is sufficient for your configuration.

Small Form Factor System

For a general-purpose SFF system, we recommend the **Antec Aria**. The Aria is inexpensive, well-built, extremely quiet, and includes a decent 300W power supply. Most important, the Aria accepts industry-standard microATX motherboards, which dramatically reduces the cost of building an SFF system. The Aria is also an excellent choice for a Home Theater PC, or for any system that needs to be small, quiet, and unobtrusive.

Other/special consideration

For a Home Theater PC system, our first choice is the **Antec Overture**, which is designed specifically for that purpose. Like the other Antec cases we recommend, the Overture is well-built and very quiet. Its height and width are comparable to standard home audio/video components, so it fits comfortably in most equipment racks and entertainment centers. Be careful about its depth, though. If your entertainment center has an enclosed back, measure carefully to ensure that the Overture is not too deep.

Avoiding bad cases

In the past, we avoided cases built in China because they were almost without exception shoddy. That's no longer true. Many good cases, including models from Antec, Lian-Li, and other top-notch companies, are now built in Chinese factories, so the country of origin is no longer the determining factor. Some companies, like Antec and Lian-Li, produce only high quality cases. Other well-known case companies, such as Enlight, produce everything from reasonably good cases at the expensive end of their product lines down to complete garbage at the cheap end. Accordingly, the best way to judge the quality of a case, assuming you can't actually examine it, is to compare its price to that of a comparable Antec case. If the other case is significantly less expensive, count on it having inferior construction quality, a poor power supply, or both. Avoid such inexpensive cases. The few dollars you save originally are more than offset by the frustrations of using a cheap case.

For updated recommendations, visit *http://www.hardwareguys.com/picks/cases.html.*

Power Supply

The power supply is one of the most important components in a PC, and yet most people give it little consideration. In addition to providing reliable, stable, closely regulated power to all system components, the power supply draws air through the system to cool it. In systems that have no supplemental fans, the power supply fan is solely responsible for exhausting the warm air inside the case at a rate high enough to prevent overheating. Figure 1-2 shows the Antec NeoPower 480, our favorite general-purpose premium power supply.

FIGURE 1-2. **The Antec NeoPower 480 power supply**

Ideally, the power supply should accomplish these tasks while producing little or no noise. Many modern power supplies, such as the Antec TruePower series and the PC Power & Cooling Silencer series, provide copious well-regulated power at minimal noise levels. In some environments, though, even that minimal noise may be unacceptable. Accordingly, power supply makers have begun producing fanless power supplies. Fanless power supplies have no moving parts, and so are silent rather than just quiet. In conjunction with a cool-running processor, a quiet (or silent) CPU cooler, and a quiet case fan, it's possible to build a PC with reasonably high performance that is nearly inaudible while running.

A marginal or failing power supply can cause many problems, some of which are very subtle and difficult to track down. For example, insufficient current on the +12V rail may harm hard drive performance by causing frequent retries when the hard drive reads or writes. Most problems are not subtle, however. A power supply that is poorly regulated or provides insufficient current causes system crashes, memory errors, and data corruption. A power supply with a failing or inadequate fan contributes to system overheating, which again causes system crashes and data corruption. In fact, many people who frequently curse Windows for its frequent crashes should instead be cursing their power supplies.

Power supply ratings are meaningless unless you understand exactly what is being rated and under what conditions. When we tell people we suspect an inadequate power supply is causing their problems, the common response is, “But it’s a <fill-in-the-brand-name> 400W unit.” We’re sure that’s true, but it doesn’t really mean much. Here’s why.

Figure 1-3 graphs the actual wattage delivered by two power supplies. The first is a PC Power & Cooling Turbo-Cool 510, which is rated at 510W. The second is a typical name-brand power supply rated at 550W. Ah, but a warm power supply delivers less wattage than a cool one. At what temperatures were they rated?

PC Power & Cooling rates its power supplies at 40° C (104° F), which is a realistic temperature for an operating power supply. Most other power supply vendors we are familiar with rate their power supplies at only 25° C (77° F). In order to deliver their rated power, these power supplies must run at 25° C, which requires an ambient room temperature below 17.5° C (60° F). Unless you keep your workspace unusually cool, a power supply rated at 25° C delivers nowhere near its rated wattage. (Antec also rates its power supplies at 40° C.)

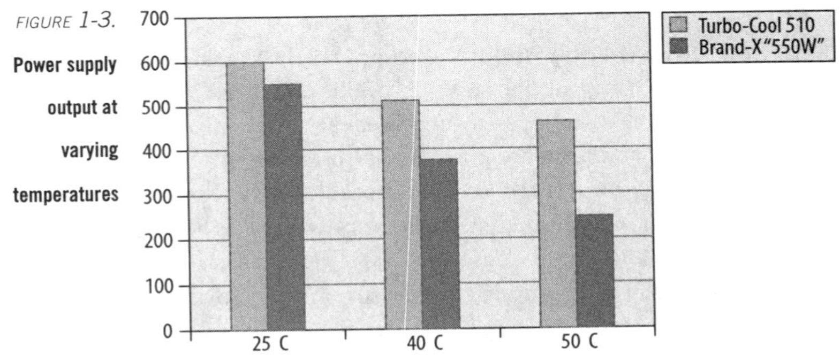

FIGURE 1-3. **Power supply output at varying temperatures**

Apples and oranges

These figures were provided by PC Power & Cooling based on their own testing, but our experience bears them out. We generally discount wattage ratings for power supplies made by companies other than PC Power & Cooling or Antec by 33%. For example, matching a 300W PC Power & Cooling or Antec power supply requires a 450W unit from most other manufacturers. How can you tell which are which? If the manufacturer doesn’t specify the temperature at which it tests and rates its power supplies, they probably use 25° C.

It’s also interesting to compare the output at varying temperatures versus the rated output. At 25° C, the Brand-X power supply delivers its rated

550W output, but the PC Power & Cooling unit, nominally rated at 510W, in fact delivers 600W, or about 118% of nominal. At 40° C, the PC Power & Cooling unit delivers its rated 510 W output, but the Brand-X unit delivers only 366W, or about 67% of nominal. At 50° C—which is the standard temperature for rating industrial PCs and is also commonly encountered during hot summer days in residential and office workspaces that are not air conditioned—the PC Power & Cooling unit delivers 460W, or about 90% of its nominal rating. At that temperature, the Brand-X unit delivers only 244W, or about 44% of its nominal rating.

The temperature at which the power supply is rated is not the only consideration in comparing power supplies. Two power supplies that have identical wattage ratings at the same temperature are not necessarily equal. That's because power supplies provide several different voltages to the motherboard and other system components, but the nominal wattage rating for a power supply lumps together the wattage ratings at different voltages. For example, Table 1-1 shows the amperage ratings and calculated wattages on various voltage rails for two 300W power supplies. (Watts are calculated by multiplying volts by amps.)

TABLE 1-1. **Two 300W power supplies compared**

	Power Supply "A"		Power Supply "B"	
Voltage Rail	**Amps**	**Watts**	**Amps**	**Watts**
+5V	30.0A	150.0W	30.0A	150.0W
+12V	12.0A	144.0W	15.0A	180.0W
-5V	0.3A	1.5W	0.5A	2.5W
-12V	1.0A	12.0W	0.5A	6.0W
+3.3V	14A	46.2W	20A	66.0W
+5Vsb	2.0A	10.0W	2.0A	10.0W
Total wattage		363.7W		414.5W
Consolidated wattage		317.5W		298.5W

The last two rows of this table give the "Total wattage" and "Consolidated wattage" for each of the power supplies. The reason for the difference is that most (but not all) power supplies specify amperage limits not just for each voltage rail, but for combinations of voltage rails. For example, Power Supply "A" can deliver 150W on the +5V rail and 46.2W on the +3.3V rail—a total of 196.2W—but the maximum combined output for those two rails is limited to 150W. Similarly, Power Supply "B" specifies a maximum combined output of 220W on the +3.3 V and +5V rails, and of 280W on the +3.3V, +5V, and +12V rails.

The amount of available current on particular voltage rails determines whether the power supply is suitable for use with particular motherboards and processors. For example, Intel Pentium 4 motherboards use +12V VRMs (voltage regulator modules) to power the processor, which means the available +12V wattage is critical. The fastest Intel Pentium 4 processors consume more than 100W, which must be provided by the +12V rail. VRMs are not 100% efficient, so the power supply must provide more +12V amperage than the nominal amount the processor requires. Also, some drive motors use +12V, which further increases the burden on the +12 V rail.

Power Supply "A" is a marginal choice for a fast Pentium 4 system—although it would be fine for a system that used a midrange Pentium 4 processor—because the 144W it provides on the +12V rail is simply too close to the combined +12V requirements of the processor and drives. This power supply would probably work even with the fastest Pentium 4 processor available, but it provides very little spare capacity.

With a 180W rating at +12V, Power Supply "B" seems to be a better choice, but that's illusory. Power Supply "A" is a PC Power & Cooling Turbo-Cool 300 with an honest 300 watts at 40° C, but Power Supply "B" is an inexpensive unit that was rated at 25° C, and so can actually deliver only perhaps 120W at +12V when operating at 40° C. The Turbo-Cool 300 is marginal for a Pentium 4/3.4 GHz or faster system, but Power Supply "B" is completely unacceptable, despite its apparently better specifications.

So what's the solution? If we were specifying a PC Power & Cooling power supply, we'd specify a Turbo-Cool 350 instead of the Turbo-Cool 300. Of that extra 50 watts, 36 watts are on the +12V rail, which is just what we need. If we were going to use a power supply made by the company that made Power Supply "B" (which we wouldn't), we'd choose another model in that series rated at 500W or 550W, which would provide output comparable to the PC Power & Cooling Turbo-Cool 350, albeit probably not as well regulated.

You want that supersized?

If you don't want to spend your time tracking down wattage requirements for each component, the best solution is to "over-buy" on the power supply. If you think a 400 watt unit will suffice, buy a 550 watt unit instead. Spending an extra $20 or $30 buys you a power supply with power to spare. Also, because that larger power supply runs at only a fraction of its rated output, it will deliver better-regulated voltage, run cooler, and last much longer. Installing a larger power

supply than you need doesn't cause the system to use more electricity. A 550W power supply that is delivering 325W uses no more power than a 350W power supply that is delivering the same 325W.

Use the following guidelines to choose a power supply appropriate for your system:

Choose the correct form factor

Above all, make sure the power supply you buy fits your case and has the proper connectors for your motherboard. Most cases use ATX power supplies, and any ATX power supply fits any ATX case. SFF and microATX cases often use SFX or proprietary power supplies. We avoid using those whenever possible.

Match power supply to system configuration

It's possible to add the maximum current draws for all system components and size the power supply on that basis. The problem with that method is that it can be nearly impossible to determine those draws for all components, especially motherboards and expansion cards. If you want to keep it simple, size your power supply according to the following configurations. (The wattages we specify are for power supplies that are rated at 40° C. For power supplies that are rated at 25° C, multiply these wattages by 1.5 or 150%.)

Basic system

For a desktop or mini-tower system with a low-end processor, 256 MB RAM, embedded video, one ATA hard disk, an ATAPI optical drive, and zero or one expansion card, install a 250W or larger ATX12V power supply.

Mainstream system

For a desktop or mini/mid-tower system with a midrange processor, 512 MB RAM, a midrange video adapter, one or two ATA hard disks, one or two ATAPI optical drives, and one or two expansion cards, install a 350W or larger ATX12V power supply.

High-performance system

For a mid- or full-tower system with a fast processor, 1 GB RAM, a high-performance video adapter, one or two SCSI or ATA hard disks, one or two optical drives, and two or more expansion cards, install a 450W or larger ATX12V power supply.

Heavily loaded system

For a full-tower system with a fast processor (or dual processors), more than 1 GB RAM, a high-performance video adapter, two or three SCSI or ATA hard disks, one or two optical drives, and three or more expansion slots filled, install a 550W or larger ATX12V power supply.

Obviously, individual configurations vary, but following these general guidelines should ensure that the power supply is adequate for the current configuration and has some room for growth if you add components. If in doubt, buy the next size up.

Dual CPUs need more power

If you build a dual-CPU system, make sure the power supply you choose is rated for dual-CPU motherboards. Even power supplies that have relatively high overall wattage ratings may not be adequate for dual-CPU motherboards. Dual processors may draw 200W or more, which may exceed the maximum allowable current at the required voltage. Our best advice for those building dual-CPU systems is to check the PC Power & Cooling web site (*http://www.pcpowercooling.com*) to locate a power supply appropriate for your configuration.

Match power supply capacity to case style

Regardless of your current configuration, take case style into account. It is senseless, for example, to install a 250W power supply in a full-tower case. You might just as well buy a smaller case, because that power supply will never support even a fraction of the number of devices the case can hold. Neither does it make sense to install a 600W power supply in a mini-tower case, which simply does not have room for enough components to require that much power.

Buy only an ATX12V-compatible power supply

Any ATX power supply you buy should meet the ATX12V specification. Pentium 4 systems require an ATX12V power supply, but even Athlon systems that do not use the ATX12V connector can use an ATX12V power supply. If you later upgrade to a motherboard that uses +12V VRMs, you will be able to use your existing power supply, assuming that it has sufficient wattage.

ATX12V main power connectors

ATX12V V2.0 power supplies have recently begun shipping. These power supplies provide a 24-pin main power connector rather than the previously standard 20-pin connector. Some 24-pin power supplies include an adapter cable that allows them to be used with a 20-pin motherboard, but it is also usually possible to connect the 24-pin main power connector to a 20-pin motherboard. Conversely, most 24-pin motherboards will accept a 20-pin main power connector, but you must usually provide supplemental power to the motherboard by connecting a hard drive power connector to it. We recommend buying only ATX12V 2.0 24-pin power supplies.

Make sure the power supply provides Serial ATA power connectors

By early 2004, many mainstream power supplies shipped with Serial ATA power connectors. Some still do not, however, so it's worth verifying that the power supply you buy includes S-ATA connectors. Even if you use Parallel (standard) ATA drives in your system, having S-ATA power connectors makes future upgrades easier. Currently, only some S-ATA hard drives require S-ATA power connectors—other S-ATA drives accept either type of connector—but in 2005 S-ATA will become increasingly ubiquitous, both for hard drives and for optical drives.

S-ATA power adapter cables

If your power supply does not provide S-ATA power connectors, you can still use it with S-ATA drives by installing S-ATA power adapter cables, such as those made by Antec (*http://www.antec-inc.com*).

What to buy

PC Power & Cooling (*http://www.pcpowercooling.com*) and Antec (*http://www.antec-inc.com*) power supplies are the Gold Standard by which we judge all other power supplies. PC Power & Cooling sells three major lines of power supplies. Their Standard series power supplies are as good as most manufacturers' best lines, although the largest unit available is only 250W. Turbo-Cool power supplies are high-performance units with extremely good regulation and high output, but they are relatively noisy. Silencer power supplies have equally good regulation, lower outputs, and are much quieter than the Turbo-Cool units. Antec premium power supplies, including the TruePower, NeoPower, and Phantom units, have regulation as good as the PC Power & Cooling units, high outputs, and are as quiet or quieter than the Silencer units. We consider the Antec premium units to be as good as the best PC Power & Cooling units.

Some brands, such as Aerocool, Enermax, Fortron, and Vantec, are well thought of amongst the enthusiast and gaming communities. We've tested several of those brands, and came away unimpressed. They're often competent enough power supplies, but offer nothing to tempt us away from PC Power & Cooling and Antec. Still others brands, like Astec and Sparkle Power, Inc. (SPI), sell primarily to system makers. Although some of these manufacturers produce competent power supplies, we see no reason to use any of them. The PC Power & Cooling units and (particularly) the Antec units are reasonably priced, stable, well-regulated, and reliable.

Cheap power supplies

Avoid cheap power supplies. There are dozens of power supply brands—many of which are made in the same Chinese and Taiwanese factories—and still other power supplies that are not branded, being marked only with required UL compliance and similar labels. Avoid entirely any power supply that is not clearly marked with the manufacturer's name. Don't assume that the power supply bundled with an inexpensive case or a $20 unit you find on the sale table at the computer store is good enough. It almost certainly isn't. A good power supply costs at least $35 for a basic system, $50 to $75 for a mainstream mini/mid-tower system, and $100 or more for heavily loaded, full-tower systems. Attempting to save money on the power supply is a false economy.

For a general-purpose system, we recommend purchasing a case that bundles one of our recommended power supplies. Otherwise, here are the power supplies we recommend.

Economy System

For an inexpensive system, use an **Antec SmartPower** power supply or a **PC Power & Cooling Standard** power supply. If you already have a case that includes a no-name power supply, we recommend replacing that cheap power supply with one of these economy units from Antec or PC Power & Cooling.

Business, Mainstream, Performance, or Gaming System

For any system for which budget is not the top priority, our first choice is the superb **Antec NeoPower** power supply. Other excellent choices are the **Antec TruePower**, the **PC Power & Cooling Turbo-Cool** (if noise level is not an issue), and the **PC Power & Cooling Silencer** models.

What does PFC mean?

PFC (Power Factor Corrected) power supplies use energy more efficiently than standard, non-PFC power supplies. PFC power supplies draw current at a steady rate, varying only according to changing loads. Non-PFC power supplies alternate drawing higher current and no current. A non-PFC power supply has maximum current draw considerably higher than an otherwise similar PFC power supply, which must be taken into account when running circuits, sizing UPSs, and so on. If you want a PFC power supply, choose one of the many PC Power & Cooling models with Active PFC or the Antec Neo-Power, which also supports Active PFC.

Gaming System

For a pure gaming system, choose an **Antec TrueBlue** or **Antec True-Control** power supply. The TrueBlue units are TruePower models with built-in blue LED illumination. The TrueControl units are TruePower models with added controls that allow you to tweak fan speed and voltages from the front panel of the computer.

FIGURE 1-4. **The fanless (and silent) Antec Phantom 350 power supply**

Quiet System

A quiet PC means different things to different people. The quietest power supplies available have no fans or other moving parts, and so are completely silent. Our favorite silent power supply is the **Antec Phantom 350**, shown in Figure 1-4, which uses a massive heatsink to cool itself. Silent power supplies are quite expensive, though. If you prefer a quiet power supply, one that is designed to use a cooling fan but produces little noise, choose an **Antec TruePower** model or a **PC Power & Cooling Silencer** model. Neither is completely silent, but both are much quieter than standard power supplies.

For updated recommendations, visit *http://www.hardwareguys.com/picks/power.html*.

Processor

If the motherboard is the heart of a computer, the processor is its brain. The processor is the most important factor to the overall performance of the system. If you use a slow processor, you end up with a slow system, no matter how fast the other components are. If you use a fast processor, you end up with a fast system, no matter how slow the other components are. That's not to say that you should blow your budget on the fastest available processor, but merely that processor speed is very significant.

AMD and Intel are the two major processor manufacturers, and account for nearly 100% of the market between them. AMD and Intel each produces two desktop processor lines, one aimed at economy systems and the other at mainstream and performance systems.

AMD Athlon 64

The Athlon 64, shown in Figure 1-5, is AMD's flagship mainstream/performance processor. The fastest Athlon 64 models have performance comparable to Intel's fastest desktop processors. The Athlon 64 is favored by serious gamers because it provides much faster gaming performance than comparably priced Intel Pentium 4 processors. Conversely, the Pentium 4 typically outperforms comparably priced Athlon 64 processors for audio/video processing and similar multimedia tasks, although the Pentium 4 has recently begun losing ground to the Athlon 64 even in that former Pentium 4 stronghold. Athlon 64 processors sell in the $150 to $900 range, and are targeted at the low-mainstream through enthusiast/gamer segments.

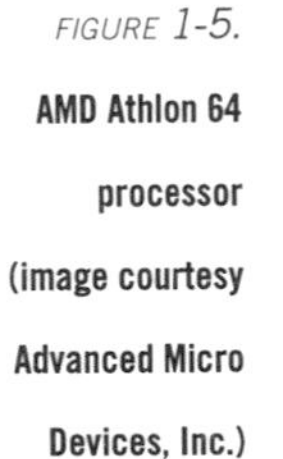

FIGURE 1-5. **AMD Athlon 64 processor (image courtesy Advanced Micro Devices, Inc.)**

AMD offers a confusing array of Athlon 64 models, with variations in clock speed, the type of socket they fit (Socket 754 versus Socket 939), the amount of Level-2 cache size (512 KB versus 1 MB), and the fabrication process (130 nm versus 90 nm). Table 1-2 shows the characteristics of current Athlon 64 processor models available as of January 2005.

TABLE 1-2. **AMD Athlon 64 processor characteristics**

Model	Frequency	L2 Cache	Fab Size	Socket
Athlon 64 FX-55	2600 MHz	1024 KB	130 nm	939
Athlon 64 FX-53	2400 MHz	1024 KB	130 nm	939
Athlon 64 FX-53	2400 MHz	1024 KB	130 nm	940
Athlon 64 FX-51	2200 MHz	1024 KB	130 nm	940
Athlon 64 4000+	2400 MHz	1024 KB	130 nm	939
Athlon 64 3800+	2400 MHz	512 KB	130 nm	939
Athlon 64 3700+	2400 MHz	1024 KB	130 nm	754
Athlon 64 3500+	2200 MHz	512 KB	130 nm	939
Athlon 64 3500+	2200 MHz	512 KB	90 nm	939
Athlon 64 3400+	2400 MHz	512 KB	130 nm	754
Athlon 64 3400+	2200 MHz	1024 KB	130 nm	754
Athlon 64 3200+	2000 MHz	1024 KB	130 nm	754
Athlon 64 3200+	2200 MHz	512 KB	130 nm	754
Athlon 64 3200+	2000 MHz	512 KB	90 nm	939
Athlon 64 3000+	2000 MHz	512 KB	130 nm	754
Athlon 64 3000+	1800 MHz	1024 KB	130 nm	754
Athlon 64 3000+	1800 MHz	512 KB	90 nm	939
Athlon 64 2800+	1800 MHz	512 KB	130 nm	754

Fabrication process size

Fabrication process size is important because, assuming the architecture remains the same, a CPU that uses a smaller process size consumes less power and runs cooler. AMD is rapidly transitioning from the older 130 nm process to the 90 nm process. Athlon 64 processors built with the 90 nm process consume considerably less power and run cooler than similar 130 nm Athlon 64 models. Intel's transition to 90 nm is nearly complete. However, because Intel made

significant architectural changes in the Pentium 4, their 90 nm (Prescott-core) models actually consume more power and run significantly hotter than their earlier 130 nm (Northwood-core) models.

Choosing among this plethora of Athlon 64 models is confusing. Several models, for example, run at the same 2400 MHz clock speed, ranging from a mainstream 3400+ model to two extremely expensive FX-53 models. Similarly, there are three models each assigned the 3000+ and 3200+ ratings, with differing clock speeds, L2 cache sizes, and sockets. In general, AMD uses the following factors to assign model ratings:

Clock speed
: All other things equal, AMD considers a 200 MHz boost in clock speed, e.g., 2000 MHz to 2200 MHz, to be one step faster. For example, a 2000 MHz Socket 754 Athlon 64 with 512 KB of L2 cache is assigned a rating of 3000+, while a similar processor operating at 2200 MHz is assigned a rating of 3200+.

Level-2 cache size
: All other things equal, AMD considers a processor with 1024 KB of L2 cache to be one step faster than a similar processor with 512 KB of L2 cache. For example, a 2000 MHz Socket 754 Athlon 64 with 512 KB of L2 cache is assigned a rating of 3000+, while a similar processor with 1024 KB of L2 cache is assigned a rating of 3200+.

Socket type
: All other things equal, AMD considers a processor that uses Socket 939 to be one step faster than a similar processor in Socket 754. For example, a 2000 MHz Socket 754 Athlon 64 with 512 KB of L2 cache is assigned a rating of 3000+, while a similar processor in Socket 939 is assigned a rating of 3200+. The justification for this is that Socket 754 processors use a 64-bit (single-channel) memory interface, while Socket 939 (and 940) processors use a 128-bit (dual-channel) memory interface.

Avoid socket 940

Socket 940 motherboards and processors are obsolescent for desktop use. They require expensive registered memory, and are being phased out quickly (although Socket 940 remains in use for server processors). If you buy an Athlon 64 processor, your first choice should be a Socket 939 model. Socket 754 models, although they

support only single-channel memory, are typically a few percentage points slower than similar Socket 939 models but cost less. AMD targets the mainstream/performance market with the Socket 939 Athlon 64 processor, and the budget market with the Socket 754 Sempron processor. AMD will gradually phase out Socket 754 Athlon 64 models in favor of Socket 939.

Two Athlon 64 processors with identical model numbers may or may not provide identical performance, depending on the applications or benchmarks you run. Applications that are more sensitive to the L2 cache size than clock speed, for example, may run faster on a 2000 MHz Athlon 64 3200+ with 1024 KB of L2 cache than on a 2200 MHz Athlon 64 3200+ with only 512 KB of L2 cache. Conversely, applications that are more sensitive to clock speed than L2 cache size may run faster on the Athlon 64 3200+ with the faster clock speed and smaller L2 cache. Overall, though, different Athlon 64 processors with the same model number typically have similar performance.

Does 64-bitness matter?

The Athlon 64 is the first mainstream desktop processor that supports 64-bit processing, although 64-bit support will remain a minor consideration for most people until 64-bit versions of Windows and major applications are available. The Athlon 64 is also a superb Intel-compatible processor when it operates in 32-bit mode.

Intel Pentium 4

The Intel Pentium 4, shown in Figure 1-6, is Intel's flagship mainstream/performance processor. By mid-2004, the transition from Intel's earlier 130 nm Northwood-core models to the 90 nm Prescott-core models was nearly complete, although Northwood-core processors are likely to remain on the market well into 2005. Intel produces Pentium 4 processors in two physical packages. The older Socket 478 remains in widespread use, although Intel is transitioning to the new Socket 775. Intel produces some Pentium 4 models for both sockets, and some for only one socket or the other. With minor exceptions, the slowest models are available only for Socket 478, the midrange models for both Socket 478 and Socket 775, and the fastest models only for Socket 775. Pentium 4 processors sell in the $150 to $1,000 range, and are targeted at the low-mainstream through enthusiast/gamer segments.

FIGURE 1-6. **Intel Pentium 4 processor (image courtesy Intel Corporation)**

Table 1-3 shows the characteristics of current Pentium 4 processor models available as of January 2005. The Pentium 4 Extreme Edition (P4/EE) processors use the older 130 nm process, and are in effect re-badged Xeon server processors. Intel introduced the P4/EE processors as a stop-gap answer to the AMD Athlon 64 FX series, which greatly outperformed the then-fastest standard Pentium 4 models. Wags claim that "EE" stands for "Extremely Expensive," and they have a point. The fastest P4/EE processors cost more than $800, as do the fastest Athlon 64 FX models. In some applications and benchmarks, they are faster than any of the mainstream models, sometimes significantly faster, but in most applications the $800 processors provide little or no performance advantage over the fastest mainstream models.

As is true of the Athlon 64, mainstream Pentium 4 processors are available in a bewildering array of models, including, for example, no less than five models that run at 2800 MHz. Pentium 4 processors are available in various combinations of CPU frequency, Front Side Bus (FSB) speed, L2 cache size, process (fab) size, and socket. If you buy a Pentium 4 processor, be very careful to order the exact model you need. Socket 775 models use the 5XX model number designation. Socket 478 models are designated by clock speed in gigahertz.

Intel "J" Processors

5XX and 5XXJ models are identical except that J-model Pentium 4 processors support the Execute Disable Bit (XDB or XDbit). XDB will be useful in the future for limiting the damage caused by viruses and other malware, but it requires operating system support, which is currently available only in newer releases of Windows and Linux. For a list of supported operating systems, see *http://www.intel.com/business/bss/infrastructure/security/xdbit.htm.* Confusingly, Intel uses

the "J" designation in different ways for the Pentium 4 and Celeron processor lines. For Pentium 4 5XX models, which are available only in Socket 775, the "J" indicates XDB support. For Celeron 3XX models, which are available in both Socket 478 and Socket 775, the "J" indicates a Socket 775 model.

TABLE 1-3. **Intel Pentium 4 processor characteristics**

Model	Frequency	FSB	L2 Cache	L3 Cache	Fab Size	Socket
Pentium 4 Extreme Edition	3400 MHz	800 MHz	512 KB	2048 KB	130 nm	478/775
Pentium 4 Extreme Edition	3200 MHz	800 MHz	512 KB	2048 KB	130 nm	478/775
Pentium 4 570J	3800 MHz	800 MHz	1024 KB	n/a	90 nm	775
Pentium 4 560/560J	3600 MHz	800 MHz	1024 KB	n/a	90 nm	775
Pentium 4 550/550J	3400 MHz	800 MHz	1024 KB	n/a	90 nm	775
Pentium 4/3.4E	3400 MHz	800 MHz	1024 KB	n/a	90 nm	478
Pentium 4 540/540J	3200 MHz	800 MHz	1024 KB	n/a	90 nm	775
Pentium 4/3.2E	3200 MHz	800 MHz	1024 KB	n/a	90 nm	478
Pentium 4/3.2C	3200 MHz	800 MHz	512 KB	n/a	130 nm	478
Pentium 4/3.06	3060 MHz	533 MHz	512 KB	n/a	130 nm	478
Pentium 4 530/530J	3000 MHz	800 MHz	1024 KB	n/a	90 nm	775
Pentium 4/3.0E	3000 MHz	800 MHz	1024 KB	n/a	90 nm	478
Pentium 4/3.0C	3000 MHz	800 MHz	512 KB	n/a	130 nm	478
Pentium 4 520/520J	2800 MHz	800 MHz	1024 KB	n/a	90 nm	775
Pentium 4/2.8E	2800 MHz	800 MHz	1024 KB	n/a	90 nm	478
Pentium 4/2.8C	2800 MHz	800 MHz	512 KB	n/a	130 nm	478
Pentium 4/2.8B	2800 MHz	533 MHz	512 KB	n/a	130 nm	478
Pentium 4/2.8A	2800 MHz	533 MHz	1024 KB	n/a	90 nm	478
Pentium 4/2.66	2660 MHz	533 MHz	512 KB	n/a	130 nm	478
Pentium 4/2.5	2500 MHz	400 MHz	512 KB	n/a	130 nm	478
Pentium 4/2.4C	2400 MHz	800 MHz	512 KB	n/a	130 nm	478
Pentium 4/2.4B	2400 MHz	533 MHz	512 KB	n/a	130 nm	478
Pentium 4/2.4A	2400 MHz	533 MHz	1024 KB	n/a	90 nm	478
Pentium 4/2.26	2260 MHz	533 MHz	512 KB	n/a	130 nm	478
Pentium 4/2.0A	2000 MHz	400 MHz	512 KB	n/a	130 nm	478

AMD Sempron

The Sempron is AMD's economy processor. It replaces the discontinued Socket A Duron processor and will soon replace the aging Socket A Athlon XP processor. In effect, Sempron processors are cut-down Athlon 64 models running at lower clock speeds with half the L2 cache—256 KB versus 512 KB or 512 KB versus 1024 KB—and no support for 64-bit processing. Various Sempron models are available in the obsolescent Socket A and in the same Socket 752 used by some Athlon 64 models. Table 1-4 shows the characteristics of current Sempron processor models available as of Janaury 2005. Sempron processors sell in the $45 to $125 range, and are targeted at the budget through low-end mainstream segment.

TABLE 1-4. **AMD Sempron processor characteristics**

Model	Frequency	L2 Cache	Fab Size	Socket
Sempron 3100+	1800 MHz	256 KB	130 nm	754
Sempron 2800+	2000 MHz	256 KB	130 nm	462 (A)
Sempron 2600+	1833 MHz	256 KB	130 nm	462 (A)
Sempron 2500+	1750 MHz	256 KB	130 nm	462 (A)
Sempron 2400+	1667 MHz	256 KB	130 nm	462 (A)
Sempron 2300+	1583 MHz	256 KB	130 nm	462 (A)
Sempron 2200+	1500 MHz	256 KB	130 nm	462 (A)

Sempron model numbers

The model numbers of Athlon 64 and Sempron processors are scaled differently. For example, the Socket 754 Sempron 3100+ runs at 1800 MHz and has 256 KB of cache, while the Socket 754 Athlon 64 2800+ runs at the same clock speed and has twice as much cache. Despite the lower model number, the Athlon 64 2800+ is somewhat faster than the Sempron 3100+. Although AMD hotly denies it, most industry observers believe that AMD intends Athlon 64 model numbers to be compared with Pentium 4 clock speeds and Sempron model numbers with Celeron clock speeds. Of course, Intel has recently abandoned designating their processors by clock speed, confusing matters even further.

Intel Celeron

Intel positions the Celeron processor for entry-level desktop systems. A Celeron processor is in effect a cut-down Pentium 4 processor, with half or a quarter as much L2 cache and a slower FSB speed. Just as AMD manages price/performance ratios to avoid allowing inexpensive Sempron processors to cannibalize sales of more profitable Athlon 64 processors, Intel is careful to set Celeron prices and performance levels to protect their Pentium 4 franchise. As is true of the Athlon 64 versus the Sempron, the fastest current Celeron is generally a bit slower than the slowest current Pentium 4, and sells for roughly the same price. Celeron processors sell in the $65 to $125 range, and are targeted at the budget through low-end mainstream segment. Table 1-5 shows athe characteristics of current Intel Celeron D processor models available as of January 2005.

Table 1-5. **Intel Celeron D processor characteristics**

Model	Frequency	FSB	L2 Cache	Fab Size	Socket
Celeron D 345/345J	3060 MHz	533 MHz	256 KB	90 nm	478/775
Celeron D 340/340J	2930 MHz	533 MHz	256 KB	90 nm	478/775
Celeron D 335/335J	2800 MHz	533 MHz	256 KB	90 nm	478/775
Celeron D 330/330J	2660 MHz	533 MHz	256 KB	90 nm	478/775
Celeron D 325/325J	2530 MHz	533 MHz	256 KB	90 nm	478/775
Celeron D 320	2400 MHz	533 MHz	256 KB	90 nm	478
Celeron D 315	2260 MHz	533 MHz	256 KB	90 nm	478

Other processors

Intel and AMD both produce other lines of processors. Intel Xeon and Itanium processors, for example, are used in servers, as are AMD Opteron processors. Similarly, both companies produce mobile processors that are targeted at notebook systems. None of these are mainstream desktop processors, and so are beyond the scope of this book.

Most people spend too much time dithering about which processor to install. The two choices you have to make are, first, Intel versus AMD, and, second, how much to spend. Here are the considerations for each of the processor price ranges:

Low-end (under $125)

Although their Celeron processors are priced in this range, Intel does not seriously compete in performance with AMD in this low-margin segment, at least at the lower end. At the bottom of this range—sub-$85 processors—inexpensive Sempron models simply mop the floor with comparably priced Celerons. The top end of this range includes processors that we consider near-mainstream models—the fastest Celerons and Semprons, midrange Athlon XPs, and the slowest Pentium 4s and Athlon 64s.

Midrange ($125 to $250)

This is the mainstream, where Intel and AMD hope to generate high volume sales because each processor they sell in this price range generates a nice profit. The bottom half of this range includes fast Athlon XPs and low-midrange Pentium 4s and Athlon 64s, either of which are good choices for a mainstream system. The top half of this range includes midrange Pentium 4s and Athlon 64s. Midrange processors as a group are generally noticeably faster than low-end processors and cost only a little more, while at the same time they are only a bit slower than high-end processors and cost a lot less. Accordingly, a midrange processor is the best choice for most systems if processor performance is at all important.

High-end ($250+)

At the lower end, $250 to $500, this range is the realm of fast Pentium 4 and Athlon 64 processors. At the high end—which may exceed $1,000—you'll find the Intel Pentium 4 Extreme Edition and the fastest Athlon 64 and Athlon 64 FX processors. This range is characterized by a rapidly decreasing bang-for-the-buck ratio. Whereas a $150 processor may be 50% faster than a $75 processor, a $400 processor may be only 10% faster than a $200 processor, and a $1,000 processor only 5% faster than a $500 one.

When speed does matter

So why would anyone spend so much more for so little additional performance? Sometimes it's worth almost any amount to improve performance even if only marginally. For example, commodities traders can make a fortune—or lose one—in literally seconds. With that much money on the line and every second critical, the $1,000 cost of the fastest processors is a trivial consideration. Similarly, if a $400 processor, or even a $1,000 one, can save a highly-paid executive only one minute a day, that processor may pay for itself in a matter of weeks, if not days.

Nor is the motivation always money. Many hardcore gamers, for example, install high-end processors because using a $1,000 processor rather than a $200 one can mean the difference between winning and losing. And then, of course, there are the bragging rights that come with having the fastest processor available.

Also consider the following issues when you choose a processor:

- Any current processor, even the slowest, is more than adequate for typical office productivity applications—web browsing, email, word processing, and similar tasks. If you never load the system heavily, you'll probably not notice any difference between an inexpensive processor and a midrange or high-end processor.

When speed doesn't matter

For example, Robert wrote an early draft of this chapter on an elderly system with a 1.7 GHz Pentium 4 processor, despite the fact that he had a dozen faster processors in his workroom, including several that were literally twice as fast as the one he was using. Why? Because the practical performance advantage of those faster processors for running OpenOffice, the Mozilla browser, and Mozilla Mail is nil. Robert can't think any faster, read any faster, or type any faster using a 3.4 GHz processor than he can using a 1.7 GHz processor. In fact, there are real advantages to using a slower processor, which consumes less power, produces less heat, and does not require fast, noisy cooling fans.

- Low-end processors (the Intel Celeron and AMD Sempron) are hampered by their small secondary caches, which are a quarter to half the size of the secondary caches used by mainstream processors. This small secondary cache may cripple performance, particularly when you are working with large data sets, such as multimedia/graphics data or video.
- In the midrange and high-end segments, Intel processors generally sell at a slight to moderate premium over AMD processors that have comparable overall performance. Intel has been able to maintain this price premium because Intel systems have historically been more stable, reliable, and compatible than AMD systems, although this Intel advantage nearly disappeared with the introduction of *n*VIDIA *n*Force-family chipsets for AMD processors. Still, the perception remains in the minds of many people that Intel is the more reliable brand, and they are accordingly willing to pay a bit more for the comfort and cachet of the Intel name.

Price the whole package

One often-overlooked factor is that Athlon 64 motherboards, particularly Socket 939 models, usually cost more than comparable Pentium 4 motherboards with similar features. Accordingly, don't judge solely on processor price. Compare the total price, including the processor and the motherboard.

- Although two processors may have similar overall performance benchmarks, that doesn't mean the processors are equal in all respects. One or the other may excel at a particular type of task. For example, comparing an Athlon 64 and a Pentium 4 with general benchmarks may show similar overall performance. But if you use a graphics or multimedia application that supports the Intel SSE-3 instruction set (which AMD processors do not support) the Intel processor may run that application literally twice as fast as the AMD processor. Someone else's benchmark results are meaningless except to the extent that those benchmarks reflect how you will use your system.

Sprint versus marathon

When it comes to multitasking, all bets are off. For example, when we benchmarked an Intel Pentium 4 against an AMD Athlon 64 that sold for about the same price, the Athlon 64 won nearly every benchmark test we ran, sometimes by significant margins. Other than graphics benchmarks that used SSE3, which the Pentium 4 won by huge margins, the Pentium 4 won few benchmarks, and those by small margins. If we believed benchmarks, we'd think the Athlon 64 was a faster processor overall. And yet, when we actually used the systems in our daily work, we found that Intel's Hyper Threading Technology paid huge dividends in real-world use. Under heavy load, with many applications running, the Pentium 4 "felt" at least as fast as the Athlon 64, and sometimes felt noticeably faster. The moral is that running benchmarks tells you how fast a system runs benchmarks, but not much else.

- There exists a "sweet spot" in the lower part of the midrange processor segment that represents the best bang-for-the-buck. Processors in this range—typically $150 to $200 for a retail-boxed processor—provide noticeably better performance than "economy" processors. Note that although the exact processor models in that price range change as Intel and AMD continually reduce prices, the sweet spot remains at about that same price level.

- In general, you should buy the processor you need initially, rather than buy a slower processor now and plan to upgrade later. The days when you could wait a year and then swap in a faster processor to double or triple system performance are long gone. Intel and AMD both make incremental performance improvements as time passes, but the fastest processor you can install in a given system is likely to be at best 25% to 50% faster than the processor already installed. This is true because Intel and AMD both have a nasty habit of changing processor sockets; older motherboards are unlikely to support the latest processors even if they use the same socket because more recent, faster processors consume more power than the older motherboard can provide.

The illusion of upgradabillity

For example, Robert's 1.7 GHz Intel Pentium 4 system uses Socket 478 (rather than the earlier Socket 423). Robert has a Socket 478 3.4 GHz Pentium 4 on his workbench, so it might seem possible to double performance simply by swapping processors. Unfortunately, the motherboard VRMs (voltage regulator modules) are not rated for the amount of current required by the 3.4 GHz processor. The fastest processor this motherboard can accept is a 2.6 GHz model, which is roughly 50% faster than the installed CPU. A 50% performance improvement is noticeable in routine use, but simply not worth the cost and effort required to upgrade given the use to which this system is put.

What to buy

Here are the processors we recommend.

Economy or Business System

For budget and business desktop systems, the **AMD Sempron** is tough to beat. It's inexpensive, reasonably fast, and (if you use the proper motherboard) stable. If you prefer an Intel-based system, choose the Socket 478 **Intel Celeron D.** In either case, order the fastest retail-boxed model you can find for $85 or so. Retail-boxed models include a suitable CPU cooler and a longer warranty than OEM (bare) models, and typically cost only a few dollars more.

Mainstream System

For mainstream systems, choose the fastest retail-boxed Socket 478 or Socket 775 **Intel Pentium 4** or Socket 754 or Socket 939 **AMD Athlon 64** you can find for $175 or so. AMD processors excel at some tasks, including gaming, and Intel processors at other tasks, including audio/video processing, but at any given price point mainstream Intel and AMD processors have performance so similar that it takes benchmark tests to show the few percentage points of difference.

Old versus new technology

Relative to Socket 775 Intel systems and Socket 939 AMD systems, Socket 478 Intel systems and Socket 754 AMD systems use older technology, provide fewer features, are somewhat slower, and are less upgradable, but cost less. If upgradability is a major consideration, choose a current Socket 939 or Socket 775 processor. To get maximum bang for your buck, choose an older Socket 754 or 478 processor.

Performance System

If processor performance is a very high priority, consider buying the fastest retail-boxed Socket 775 **Intel Pentium 4** or Socket 939 **AMD Athlon 64** you can find for $300 or so, but think hard before you spend that extra money. Relative to mainstream $175 processors, a $300 processor provides only marginally faster performance. A system with the more expensive processor will feel "snappier" and run CPU-intensive tasks perceptibly faster, but only just. We think the $125 or so extra that such a processor costs is usually better spent elsewhere, such as on a better display or video adapter or more memory. Once the cost of the processor exceeds $200 or so, it becomes a matter of rapidly diminishing returns.

The reality of upgradability

We mentioned earlier that we recommend buying the processor you need now, rather than planning to upgrade later. That's true for most systems, but for a performance system we think it's usually better to "split" your processor purchase money in two. Buy a mainstream $150 or $175 processor initially and replace it in a year or 18 months with a new mainstream $150 or $175 processor rather than spend $300 or $350 initially on a performance processor and use that processor for two or three years. The $300 processor will be a bit faster than mainstream initially, but as faster processors become available the $300 processor will quickly drop to mainstream and then entry-level performance levels. Conversely, replacing the $175 processor after 18 months with a then-mainstream $175 processor gives the system a mid-life boost at the same overall cost.

Gaming System

For a budget gaming system, choose the fastest retail-boxed Socket 754 **AMD Sempron** you can find for $125 or so. For a mainstream gaming system, our first choice would be the fastest retail-boxed **AMD Athlon 64** we could find for $175 or so, although a similarly-priced **Intel Pentium 4** is also a good choice, particularly if the system is also used for other purposes. For a dedicated gaming system on a larger budget, we'd choose one of the $300 performance processors. A fast AMD Athlon 64 would be our first choice, but a fast Intel Pentium 4 is also acceptable. For gaming, even an incremental boost in processor performance can be worth the additional cost. Finally, for a cost-no-object dedicated gaming system, we'd choose the fastest **AMD Athlon 64 FX** we could find. The Intel Pentium 4/EE simply can't compete with the Athlon 64 FX for a gaming system.

Quiet System

For a quiet system, choose the slowest processor that is fast enough for your requirements. Faster processors produce more heat and require faster (and noisier) cooling fans. If quiet operation and processor performance are both important, use a 90 nm **AMD Athlon 64** processor. These models are fast but produce significantly less heat than current Intel desktop processors. Also consider the processor core type and speed if you are building a quiet system. Some quiet CPU coolers, such as the Zalman "flower" series units, can be run in fanless mode if you use a cool-running processor, for example a Northwood-core Pentium 4/2.8 or slower. The processor core stepping is another consideration. For example, early steppings of the Prescott-core Pentium 4 run very hot, while the most recent steppings run considerably cooler. Using a cooler-running processor allows you to minimize or eliminate the fan noise generated by the CPU cooler, so it's an important consideration if your goal is to build a quiet PC.

Linux System

If you run desktop Linux, particularly a distribution that does not use the latest kernel and drivers, choose a Socket 478 **Intel Celeron D** or **Intel Pentium 4** processor. The issue is not processor compatibility *per se*, but motherboard and chipset compatibility. Linux lags Windows somewhat in supporting recent components such as Intel 9XX and *n*VIDIA *n*Force3 and *n*Force4 chipsets, PCI Express, and so on. Although it may be possible to get a recent Linux distro—particularly a bleeding-edge distro such as Gentoo—running on very recent hardware, it is generally much easier to use mainstream hardware. Even if your distro isn't quite bleeding-edge, you may be able to run a bleeding-edge kernel with support for your hardware (see *http://www.kernel.org* for the latest kernel releases). Of course, adventurous folks who don't mind rebuilding their kernels can have it all—the latest kernel features and support for bleeding-edge hardware.

For updated recommendations, visit *http://www.hardwareguys.com/picks/processors.html.*

Heatsink/Fan Unit (CPU cooler)

Modern processors consume 50W to 100W or more. That power must be dissipated as heat. In effect, a modern system has the equivalent of a 50W to 100W incandescent light bulb burning at all times inside the case. In reality, that understates the problem. A light bulb dissipates 50W to 100W from the relatively large surface of the bulb. A processor must dissipate the same amount of heat over the much smaller surface area of the processor die, typically about 0.25 square inches. Without an effective heatsink to draw away this heat, the processor might literally burn itself to a crisp almost instantly.

Nearly all systems deal with this heat problem by placing a massive metal heatsink in close contact with the processor die (or integrated heat spreader) and using a small fan to draw air through the heatsink fins. This device is called a heatsink/fan (HSF) or CPU cooler. As the power dissipation of processors has continued growing, so too has the size and mass of the heatsinks they use. Figure 1-7 shows Robert removing the protective plastic from the base of the HSF supplied with a retail-boxed Pentium 4 560 processor.

FIGURE 1-7. **Removing the protective plastic from a Pentium 4 560 CPU cooler**

Danger, Will Robinson!

Do not assume merely because a heatsink fits a processor that it is sufficient to cool that processor. Faster processors are physically identical to slower models, but produce more heat. Heatsinks are rated by processor speed. For example, a heatsink rated for a 2.4 GHz Pentium 4 can physically be installed on a 3.4 GHz Pentium 4, but is grossly inadequate to cool it. Nor can you judge solely by processor speed. For example, Intel has produced 2.8 GHz Pentium 4 processors using the earlier, cooler—running Northwood core and the current, hotter running Prescott core. A heatsink rated for use with a 2.8 GHz Northwood-core Pentium 4 is not good enough for a 2.8 GHz Prescott-core Pentium 4. Make sure that the heatsink/fan unit you choose is rated for the specific processor you use it with.

Heatsinks are constructed with different materials, according to their prices and intended uses. An inexpensive heatsink, or one intended for use with a slower processor, is likely to be of all-aluminum construction. Aluminum is inexpensive and relatively efficient in transferring heat. Copper is much more expensive than aluminum, but is also much more efficient in transferring heat. Accordingly, a more expensive heatsink, or one intended for a faster processor, might be constructed primarily of aluminum, but with copper surfaces where the processor contacts the heatsink. The most expensive heatsinks, and those intended for use with the fastest processors, are constructed of pure copper.

Heatsink/fan units also differ in the type and size of fan they use, and how fast that fan runs. Fan speed is an issue because, all other things being equal, a faster-running fan produces more noise. For equal air flow, a larger, slower fan produces less noise than a smaller, faster fan. Fan sizes have increased as processor speeds increased, to provide the high air flow volume needed to cool the heatsink while keeping fan speed (and noise) at a reasonable level. For example, heatsinks for Pentium II processors used 30 mm fans. Heatsinks for current Pentium 4 and Athlon 64 processors typically use 60 mm or 70 mm fans. Some third-party "performance" heatsinks targeted at overclockers use 80 mm, 92 mm, or 120 mm fans. Some even use multiple fans.

Don't forget the goop

The best heatsink/fan can't cool a processor properly unless thermal compound is used at the processor/heatsink interface. The processor and heatsink base are both flat and polished, but even when they

are pressed into close contact, a thin layer of air separates them. Air insulates well, which is the last thing you want, so thermal compound is used to displace the air.

When you install a heatsink, and each time you remove and replace it, use fresh thermal compound to ensure proper heat transfer. Thermal compound is available in the form of viscous thermal "goop" and as phase-change thermal pads, which melt as the processor heats up and solidify as it cools down. Make sure that the thermal compound you use is approved by the processor maker. For example, AMD specifies particular phase-change thermal pads for certain of its processors, and warns that using any other thermal compound voids the warranty.

What to buy

In general, we recommend using the heatsink/fan units that are bundled with retail-boxed processors. Processors are generally available in OEM versions, which have short warranties and no heatsink/fan unit, and in retail-boxed versions that have much longer warranties and include a heatsink/fan unit certified by the manufacturer. Retail-boxed processors typically sell for only a few dollars more than OEM models, so it's often actually less expensive to buy the retail-boxed processor than to buy an OEM model and a separate heatsink/fan unit. The bundled heatsink/fan units are generally midrange in terms of performance and noise level—neither as efficient nor as quiet as the best third-party units.

If you choose not to use a bundled HSF, here are the heatsink/fan units we recommend.

Economy System

If you use an OEM processor and need an inexpensive CPU cooler, choose a unit made by Dynatron (*http://www.dynatron-corp.com*).

Quiet System

If you need a very quiet heatsink/fan unit, we recommend the following products:

For Socket A, our first choices are the **Zalman CNPS7000A-Cu,** the **Zalman CNPS7000A-AlCu,** or the **Thermalright SP-97**. The **Thermalright SLK-900A** is also a good choice (*http://www.zalmanusa.com* or *http://www.thermalright.com*).

For AMD K8 processors (Sockets 754, 939, or 940) our first choice is the **Thermalright XP-120** and our second choice the **Thermalright XP-90**. The **Zalman CNPS7000B-Cu** or the **Zalman CNPS7000B-AlCu** is also a good choice.

For Socket 478 processors, our first choice is the **Thermalright XP-120** and our second choice the **Thermalright XP-90**. The **Zalman CNPS7000B-Cu** or the **Zalman CNPS7000B-AlCu** is also a good choice, as is the **Thermalright SP-94**.

For Socket 775 processors, our first choice is the all-copper **Zalman CNPS7700-Cu** and our second choice the aluminum-copper **Zalman CNPS7700-AlCu**. These massive units can cool any current processor efficiently, including the hot-running Pentium 4 570. The all-copper unit can cool any current processor in what Zalman calls "Silent Mode", which means the CPU fan runs at 1,000 to 1,400 RPM. The aluminum-copper model can use Silent Mode through the Pentium 4 540, but uses "Low-noise Mode" (1,400 to 2,000 RPM) for faster processors. Either of these CPU coolers also works well for any AMD Socket 754, 939, or 940 processor, as well as all Socket 478 Intel models.

The best thermal compound

As for thermal transfer medium, we generally use the thermal compound or phase-change medium that is provided with the heatsink/fan unit, assuming it is approved by the processor maker. (AMD in particular is very specific about which thermal transfer media are acceptable for its processors.) When we remove and reinstall a heatsink/fan, we generally use Antec Silver Thermal Compound (*http://www.antec-inc.com*), which is as good as or better than anything else we've used, and sells for a fraction of the price of the "premium" silver thermal compounds.

Cheap and expensive CPU coolers

Do not under any circumstances use one of the generic "no-name" heatsink/fan units you find on the bargain tables in some computer stores or computer fairs. We've seen these for as little as $3 or $4, with the CPU rating written on the box with a felt-tip pen. Anyone who'd install a no-name $4 heatsink/fan on a $200 processor probably deserves whatever happens.

At the opposite extreme, we recommend avoiding the premium heatsink/fan units that are so beloved by overclockers. You can easily spend $75 or more on such a unit, and it will provide little or no cooling benefit relative to the stock heatsink/fan or an inexpensive Dynatron unit. For example, we tested an $18 Dynatron unit against a "big-name" unit that sold for $58, using the same processor and thermal compound. The results? The CPU temperature with the Dynatron stabilized at 33° C, versus 32° C with the premium unit. BFD.

For updated recommendations, visit *http://www.hardwareguys.com/picks/processors.html.*

The Wrong HSF Can Kill Your Motherboard

Choosing the best aftermarket HSF is not trivial. Verifying that the HSF is rated for your particular processor is just the first step. Specialty HSFs—those that provide high cooling efficiency or low noise levels, or both—are typically large and heavy (and expensive).

Size is important because the space around the processor socket is often cluttered with capacitors and other components that may prevent a large HSF from being seated properly. More than one system builder has learned to his dismay that an HSF that appears to fit may—upon being clamped down—bend, damage, or short out nearby components. We have never understood why most third-party HSF makers don't provide motherboard compatibility lists (Zalman, for one, does). In the absence of such lists, the best way to avoid damaging your motherboard is to verify visually that all components will clear the HSF before you clamp it into place. If it doesn't fit—well, that's another good argument for buying from vendors that have good return policies.

Weight is important because Intel and AMD specify maximum heatsink weights for which the retaining brackets for their various processors are rated. An Intel Pentium III heatsink, for example, can weigh no more than 180 grams, and an AMD Socket A heatsink no more than 300 grams. Most specialty HSF units exceed the maximum allowable weight—sometimes by large margins—which introduces the ugly possibility of the HSF breaking free from its mount and

continued

rattling around loose inside the case. This is an issue with any tower system or other PC that mounts the motherboard vertically, and is a particular danger with portable systems, such as LAN party PCs. AMD Athlon Socket A systems are particularly prone to this problem because the HSF clamps to the CPU socket directly rather than to a retaining bracket that is secured to the motherboard.

The best solution, if you must use such a heavy HSF, is to choose one that comes with a custom retaining bracket rather than depending on the standard motherboard bracket.

Motherboard

The motherboard is the main logic board around which a PC is built. The motherboard is the center of the PC in the sense that every system component connects to the motherboard, directly or indirectly. The motherboard provides sockets or slots for the processor and memory, interfaces for drives, various communications ports, and many other features, all of which are controlled by the motherboard.

Because the motherboard is the heart of the system, it pays to select it carefully. The motherboard you choose determines which processors are supported, how much and what type of memory the system can use, what type of video adapters can be installed, the speed of the communication ports, and many other key system characteristics. The motherboard is usually the most expensive system component except possibly the processor, so choosing the wrong motherboard can be a costly mistake.

Use the following guidelines when choosing a motherboard:

Decide which processor to use

The processor you choose determines the type of motherboard you need. For a Pentium 4 or Celeron system, choose a Socket 478 (current technology) or Socket 775 (the new Socket T) motherboard. The former are less expensive and more widely available; the latter incorporate newer chipsets, provide additional features such as PCI Express support and provide a better upgrade path. For an Athlon XP system, choose a Socket A motherboard. For a Sempron system, choose a Socket A or Socket 754 motherboard, according to the processor packaging of the Sempron processor you want to use. For an Athlon 64 system, choose a Socket 939 motherboard.

Buy a motherboard that uses the right chipset

For a Pentium 4 or Celeron processor, choose a motherboard that uses an Intel 865- or 875-series chipset (for Socket 478) or an Intel 9-series chipset (for Socket T), depending on your budget and priorities. For a Socket A Athlon XP or Sempron processor, choose a motherboard that uses an *n*VIDIA *n*Force2-series chipset. For a Socket 754 or Socket 939 Sempron or Athlon 64 processor, choose a motherboard that uses an *n*VIDIA *n*Force3-series or *n*Force4-series chipset.

Make sure the motherboard supports the exact processor you plan to use

Just because a motherboard claims to support a particular processor doesn't mean it supports all members of that processor family. For example, some motherboards support the Pentium 4 processor, but only slower models. Other motherboards support fast Pentium 4s, but not slower Pentium 4s or Celerons. Similarly, some motherboards support the Athlon with a 200, 266, or 333 MHz FSB, but not the 400 MHz FSB. As Intel and AMD transition to Socket T and Socket 939, respectively, they are shipping processors that are identical to older models except for the socket they fit. If you have a Socket T 3.4 GHz Pentium 4, a Socket 478 motherboard is of no use to you, and vice versa.

Check processor compatibility

Make sure the motherboard supports the *exact* processor you plan to use, before you buy it. To do so, visit the motherboard manufacturer's web site and look at the "supported processors" page for the exact motherboard you plan to use. Note that motherboard makers often "slipstream" revised models with the same model number, and the list of supported processors almost always assumes you are using the current motherboard revision. Quite often, an earlier revision does not support all of the processor models or speeds supported by a later revision. When you buy a motherboard, make sure to get the latest available revision.

Choose a board with flexible host bus speeds

Choose a motherboard that supports at least the settings you need now and expect to need for the life of the board. For example, even if you install a 400 MHz FSB Celeron initially, you should choose a motherboard that supports Pentium 4 processors using the 400, 533, and 800 MHz FSB speeds. Similarly, even if you plan to install an inexpensive 266 MHz FSB Athlon at first, choose a motherboard that supports the full range of Athlon FSB speeds—200, 266, 333, and 400 MHz. Boards that offer a full range of host-bus speeds, ideally in small increments, give you the most flexibility. If you intend to overclock your system, make sure the motherboard offers multiple choices of host-bus speed (again, the smaller the increments, the better) and allows you to set CPU voltage, ideally over a wide range in 0.05 volt increments.

Make sure the board supports the type and amount of memory you need
Any motherboard you buy should support PC3200 DDR-SDRAM or DDR2. Do not make assumptions about how much memory a motherboard supports. A motherboard has a certain number of memory slots and the literature may state that it accepts memory modules up to a specific size, but that doesn't mean you can necessarily install the largest supported module in all of the memory slots. For example, a motherboard may have four memory slots and accept 512 MB DIMMs, but you may find that you can use all four slots only if you install 256 MB DIMMs. Memory speed may also come into play. For example, a particular motherboard may support three or four PC2700 modules, but only two PC3200 modules.

Check memory compatibility

Don't assume that you can use all available memory slots. For example, many early Socket 754 Athlon 64 motherboards provided three or even four DIMM slots, but could actually support only two memory modules reliably, regardless of the size or speed of those modules. Nor do all motherboards necessarily support the full amount of memory that the chipset itself supports, even if there are sufficient memory sockets available. Always check to determine exactly what combinations of memory sizes, types, and speeds are supported by a particular motherboard.

For a general-purpose system, support for 1 GB of RAM is acceptable. For a system that will be used for memory-intensive tasks such as professional graphics, make sure the motherboard supports at least 2 GB of RAM.

Don't salvage old memory

Although you may be able to find a new motherboard that allows you to migrate existing memory from your old motherboard, it's usually not a good idea to do so unless that older memory is current—i.e., PC3200 DDR-SDRAM. Memory is cheap, and it makes little sense to base a new motherboard purchase decision on the ability to salvage a relatively small amount of old, slow, cheap memory.

Check documentation, support, and updates

Before you choose a motherboard, check the documentation and support that's available for it, as well as the BIOS and driver updates available. Some people think that a motherboard that has many patches and updates available must be a bad motherboard. Not so. Frequent patch and update releases indicate that the manufacturer takes support seriously. We recommend to friends and clients that they give great weight to—and perhaps even base their buying decisions on—the quality of the web site that supports the motherboard.

Buy a motherboard with the proper form factor

If you are building a new system, choose an ATX motherboard that best meets your needs, and then buy an ATX case and power supply to hold it. For most purposes, a full-size ATX motherboard is the best choice. If system size is a major consideration, a microATX or FlexATX motherboard may be a better choice, although using the smaller form factor has several drawbacks, notably giving up several expansion slots and making it more difficult to route cables and cool the system.

The preceding issues are always important in choosing a motherboard. But there are many other motherboard characteristics to keep in mind. Each of them may be critical for some users and of little concern to others. These characteristics include:

Expansion slots

Any motherboard provides PCI expansion slots, but motherboards differ in how many slots they provide. Three slots is marginal, four adequate, and five or more preferable. Integrated motherboards—those with embedded video, sound, and/or LAN—can get by with fewer slots. Having an AGP 3.0 slot (8X) is a definite plus, even if the motherboard includes embedded video.

PCI express slots

New-generation motherboards, those based on Intel 9XX and nVIDIA nForce4 chipsets, provide PCI Express (PCIe) expansion slots in addition to PCI slots and instead of an AGP slot. These motherboards typically provide one x16 PCIe slot, which accepts a PCIe graphics adapter, and one or two x1 PCIe slots. The x1 PCIe slots are intended for standard expansion cards, such as network adapters or audio adapters, but PCIe adapters are not yet commonly available. PCIe graphics adapters, however, are readily available now.

Warranty

It may seem strange to give so little weight to warranty, but the truth is that warranty should not be a major consideration for most users. Motherboards generally work or they don't. If a motherboard is going to fail, it will likely do so right out of the box or within a few days of use. In practical terms, the vendor's return policy is likely to be more important than the manufacturer's warranty policy. Look for a vendor who replaces DOA motherboards quickly, preferably by cross-shipping the replacement.

Ports and connectors

At a minimum, the motherboard should provide four or more USB 2.0 ports—six or eight is better—and a dual ATA/100 or faster hard disk interface. Ideally the motherboard should also provide at least two Serial ATA connectors, and four is better. (Some motherboards with four S-ATA connectors include only one parallel ATA interface, which is acceptable.) We also like to have a serial port, an EPP/ECP parallel port, a PS/2 keyboard port, a PS/2 mouse port, and an FDD interface, but those "legacy" ports are fast disappearing, replaced by USB.

Embedded sound, video, and LAN

Some motherboards include embedded sound, video, and/or LAN adapters as standard or optional equipment. In the past, such motherboards were often designed for low-end systems, and used inexpensive and relatively incapable audio and video components. But nowadays many motherboards include very capable audio, video, and LAN adapters, making them good choices around which to build a mainstream midrange system. Such motherboards normally cost from $0 to $25 or so more than similar motherboards without the embedded peripherals, allowing you to save $50 to $150 by buying the integrated motherboard rather than separate components. If you buy such a motherboard, make sure that the embedded devices can be disabled if you later want to replace the embedded adapters with better components.

The downside to embedded features

Embedded adapters often use the main CPU, which can reduce performance by a few percent. The speed of current processors means this is seldom an issue. However, if processor performance is critical, you may wish to use a motherboard that has few or no embedded functions.

Embedded Gigabit Ethernet is a particular concern. If you buy a motherboard with embedded Gigabit Ethernet, make sure it uses a dedicated communications channel, such as the Communications Streaming Architecture (CSA) channel used by Intel chipsets or a PCIe channel. Some inexpensive motherboards have embedded Gigabit Ethernet adapters that connect via the PCI bus. That's a problem because Gigabit Ethernet is fast enough to saturate the PCI bus.

Power management and system management

We regard power management as a useless feature and do not use it. It saves little power, increases the wear and tear on the equipment due to frequent power cycling, and tends to cause bizarre incompatibilities. We have experienced numerous problems with ACPI, with many different motherboards and operating systems, including systems that go into a coma rather than going to sleep, requiring a hard reboot to recover, and so recommend not using it at all. If for some reason you need power management, make sure the motherboard you buy supports at least a subset of the ACPI specification. Most current motherboards support some ACPI functions, but determining exactly which requires detailed examination of the technical documents for that motherboard.

System management is usually unimportant outside a corporate environment. If system management is an issue for you, look for a motherboard that supports all or some of the following features: voltage monitoring, CPU and/or system temperature sensors, a chassis intrusion alarm, and fan activity monitoring for one or more fans.

Wakeup functions

Again, these features are primarily of interest to corporate IS folks rather than individual users. But if wakeup functions are important to you, you can buy a motherboard that supports "Wake-on" some or all of the following: LAN activity, modem ring-in, keyboard/mouse activity, and real-time clock.

Boot device support

Any motherboard supports booting from the hard drive or a floppy drive. Most motherboards also support booting from El Torito compliant CD-ROM drives and from floppy-replacement drives like the LS-120 or Zip Drive. Some motherboards support booting from the network. If boot support is an issue for you, make sure the motherboard you buy supports booting from your preferred device. Also make sure that CMOS Setup allows you to specify a boot sequence that lets you to make your preferred device the primary boot device.

What to buy

Here are the motherboards we recommend.

Economy or Business System

For an economy or corporate system, the goal is a reasonably inexpensive board that is extremely reliable. Embedded video, audio, and LAN adapters usually suffice, and allow you to cut costs without reducing reliability.

For a Socket 478 Celeron or Pentium 4 system, our first choice is the **Intel D865GBFL**. The build quality is very high, and the board is fast and as stable as any we've used. The embedded video, audio, and LAN are more than good enough for nearly any purpose. The **Intel D865PERL** is essentially a D865GBFL without embedded video, and is equally good. Choose the D865PERL if you want to install a separate AGP 3D graphics adapter. For a Socket 775 Celeron or Pentium 4 system, choose the **Intel D915GAGL** (microATX) or **D915GAVL** (ATX) motherboard. Both have Intel's typical top-notch build quality, use standard PC3200 DDR-SDRAM rather than expensive DDR2 memory, and have excellent embedded video, audio, and LAN.

For a Socket A Athlon XP or Sempron system, choose the **ASUS A7N8X-VM/400**, which provides decent embedded video, audio, and LAN functions, and has an AGP slot for those who prefer to use a separate video adapter. For a Socket 754 Sempron or Athlon 64 system, we know of no motherboards with embedded video that we can recommend, but the **ASUS K8N** is inexpensive, fast, fully featured, and has excellent build quality. Coupled with an inexpensive AGP video adapter, the ASUS K8N is an excellent choice for an economy or corporate Socket 754 system.

Mainstream System

For a mainstream Pentium 4 system, choose the Socket 775 **Intel D915PGNL** or **D915PBLL** with a mainstream PCIe video adapter, or the Socket 478 **Intel D865PERL** with a mainstream AGP video adapter. For a mainstream Athlon 64 system, our first choice in Socket 754 is the **ASUS K8N-E Deluxe** with a mainstream AGP video adapter, and in Socket 939 the **ASUS A8N-SLI Deluxe** with a mainstream PCIe video adapter.

Performance System

For a performance Pentium 4 system, choose the Socket 775 **Intel D925XCV** with a performance PCIe video adapter, or the Socket 478 **Intel D875PBZ** with a performance AGP video adapter. For a performance Athlon 64 system, choose the Socket 939 **ASUS A8N-SLI Deluxe** with a performance PCIe video adapter.

Gaming System

For a budget gaming system, choose the Socket 754 **ASUS K8N** with a Sempron or inexpensive Athlon 64 processor.

For a mainstream gaming system, choose the **ASUS K8N-E Deluxe** (Socket 754), the **ASUS A8N-SLI Deluxe** (Socket 939), the **Intel D865PERL** (Socket 478), or the **Intel D915PGN** (Socket 775).

For a performance gaming system, if you prefer Intel processors, choose the **Intel D875PBZ** (Socket 478) or the **Intel D925XCV** (Socket 775). If you prefer AMD processors, which we recommend for gaming systems, choose the Socket 939 **ASUS A8N-SLI Deluxe.** The ASUS A8N-SLI Deluxe allows you to install two PCIe video adapters and use both simultaneously for gaming. For example, you can install two $200 nVIDIA 6000-series PCIe video adapters that provide better overall video performance in many games than one $600 adapter. Of course, if you want the ultimate gaming system, you can install two $600 video adapters.

Our preferred manufacturers

Over the years, we've come to have strong preferences in motherboard brands, based on build quality, compatibility, frequency of driver/BIOS updates, and similar factors. We consider Intel and ASUS to be the only first-tier motherboard makers, and choose their products whenever possible. At times, for one reason or another, we've used motherboards from Aopen, EPoX, Gigabyte, MSI (Microstar), Super Micro, and Tyan, with generally good results, but those brands are always our second choice. We avoid motherboards from ABIT, Adtran, Albatron, Biostar, Chaintech, DFI, ECS (Elitegroup Computer Systems), FIC, Iwill, Leadtek, Shuttle, Soyo, Vantec, and others we haven't listed. We also avoid motherboards, even those made by our preferred manufacturers, that use certain chipsets. For Intel CPUs, we use motherboards that are built on Intel chipsets. For AMD CPUs, we use motherboards that are based on *n*VIDIA *n*Force chipsets. In particular, based on numerous bad experiences over the years, we

avoid any motherboard that uses a VIA Technologies chipset or a PC Chips chipset. We have on occasion used motherboards based on ALi and SiS chipsets, but in general we avoid them as well.

For updated recommendations, visit *http://www.hardwareguys.com/picks/motherboards.html.*

Our personal systems

So, what do we actually use? In Janaury 2005, we did a quick inventory of our home systems and found:

- **Pentium 4/3.2 in an Intel D865GBF (Barbara, primary office system, Xandros Linux)**
- **Sempron 3100+ in an ASUS K8N-E Deluxe (Barbara, secondary office system, Windows XP)**
- **Pentium 4/3.0 in an Intel D865GRH (Robert, primary office system, Xandros Linux)**
- **Pentium 4 560 in an Intel D925XCV (Robert, secondary office system, Windows XP)**
- **Pentium 4/EE 3.4 in an Intel D875PBZ (gaming system)**
- **Athlon 64 FX-53 in an ASUS A8N-SLI Deluxe (gaming system)**
- **Pentium 4/3.2 in an Intel D865PERL (Robert, den system)**
- **Athlon XP 2600+ in an ASUS A7N8X-E Deluxe (PVR system)**
- **Sempron 2800+ in an ASUS A7N8X-VM/400 (test-bed system)**
- **Athlon 64 3500+ in an ASUS A8V Deluxe (test-bed system)**

Of course, there are also numerous other servers, test-bed systems, and so on, and things do change quickly around here.

Memory

Installing sufficient memory of the proper type is critical to system performance. Fortunately, memory is inexpensive enough nowadays that even entry-level systems can be equipped with sufficient memory without breaking the bank.

Although Intel is pushing DDR2 memory with their new 9-series chipsets, standard PC3200 DDR-SDRAM is still the mainstream memory technology, and is likely to remain so for some time. Although DDR2 memory will eventually become mainstream, its short-term prospects are poor because it currently costs more and is slower than PC3200 DDR-SDRAM. Tastes terrible, more filling. For now, PC3200 DDR-SDRAM is the safe bet.

The only real decisions are how much memory to install and what size modules to use. For entry-level systems, we recommend no less than 256 MB, although Windows XP is happier with more. For mainstream systems, 512 MB may suffice, depending on the application mix, but 1 GB is often advisable. For performance systems, workstations, and multimedia/graphics systems, install at least 1 GB, and more is usually better. Consider the following factors when choosing memory modules:

Price per megabyte
: In general, it's less expensive to buy a given amount of memory in one module rather than two or more modules. For example, if you are installing 256 MB, a single 256 MB DIMM will probably cost less than two 128 MB DIMMs, sometimes much less. Conversely, the largest capacity modules often sell at a substantial premium. For example, a 1 GB DIMM may cost three times as much as a 512 MB DIMM, rather than only twice as much.

Motherboard memory support
: Not all motherboards support all DIMM capacities. For example, some motherboards may support 256 MB DIMMs, but not 512 MB DIMMs. The allowable mix may also differ. For example, one motherboard may support 512 MB DIMMs in all four of its memory slots. Another may support 512 MB DIMMs in only two of its four slots, and require that you leave the other two slots vacant or install 256 MB or smaller DIMMs in those slots. Still another may support a maximum of 1 GB of RAM using 512 MB DIMMs, requiring you to leave two of its four memory slots vacant if you install 512 MB DIMMs in the first two slots.

ECC versus non-parity modules
: Memory modules are produced in two varieties. Non-parity modules are 64 bits wide, and provide no error detection or correction. ECC modules are 72 bits wide, and use the extra 8 bits to store error detection and correction data. ECC modules can detect and correct all single-bit errors. ECC modules can detect all multi-bit errors, and correct some of them. This error detection and correction has two prices: ECC modules cost 8% to 15% more than non-parity modules, and the ECC circuitry imposes a performance penalty of a few percent. In the past, ECC modules were used primarily in servers, where the benefits were worth the costs. We recommend using ECC memory in standard PCs only if you install more than 2 GB of memory. For 2 GB or less, use

non-parity modules. (Note that ECC requires chipset support. If you install ECC memory in a system whose chipset does not support ECC, the ECC modules usually work properly, but only as standard non-parity modules.)

Registered versus unbuffered DIMMs
Registered DIMMs have additional circuitry that "hides" the actual memory chips from the chipset memory controller. Because memory controllers are limited in how many memory devices (chips) they can support, using registered memory allows the controller to support more memory than it otherwise could. The downside is that registered DIMMs cost more than unbuffered (standard) DIMMs and are slower. Some motherboards, typically multi-processor and server models, require registered DIMMs. If you build a system around such a motherboard, buy registered DIMMs that are certified compatible with your motherboard. Otherwise, use standard unbuffered DIMMs.

CAS Latency (CL)
Memory performance can differ even between memory modules of the same general speed class. For example, PC3200 memory is available in standard CL3 versions and in faster CL2.5 versions. The difference has to do with how long the processor must wait before the memory begins delivering data it requested. Standard CL3 memory uses 4-3-3-3 memory timings. CL2.5 memory supports faster 3-3-3-3 memory timings. The performance advantage of CL2.5 memory varies according to the type of memory access being used—the faster memory helps more for random memory accesses than sequential memory accesses—but is typically close to 3%. Note that this is a 3% advantage in *memory* performance, not in overall system performance. Memory performance is only one aspect of overall system performance, so using CL2.5 memory seldom provides any real performance benefit. If CL2.5 memory is available for the same price as CL3 memory, we'll choose the faster memory, but we won't pay any price premium for it.

What to buy

We use Crucial and Kingston memory in nearly all of our systems, and recommend others do the same. Crucial is vertically integrated. They start literally with sand and produce finished memory modules. Kingston is an assembler, which means they don't actually produce memory chips. Instead, they buy memory chips from Crucial and other top-notch manufacturers, and assemble those chips carefully into first-rate memory modules. Kingston produces two lines of memory. Their ValueRAM modules are top-notch general-purpose memory. Their HyperX modules support faster than standard memory timings, and are useful in applications where memory performance is critical. Here are the memory modules we recommend.

Economy, Business, or Mainstream System

For economy, business/corporate, and mainstream systems, we recommend **Crucial PC3200 DDR-SDRAM** or Kingston **PC3200 DDR-SDRAM.** Both companies have "configurators" on their websites that allow you to specify the make and model of your motherboard and obtain a list of memory modules that are compatible with that motherboard.

Performance or Gaming System

Although we do not recommend "performance" memory for most systems, it may make sense to buy premium memory for a performance or gaming system, particularly if you plan to overclock it. Our first choice in premium DDR memory is **Crucial Ballistix PC3200. Kingston HyperX** is also a good choice, as is **OCZ 3500EB** or **OCZ 3700EB.** For DDR2 modules, we have used only **Crucial PC2-4200U**, although Corsair, Kingmax, Mushkin, and OCZ DDR2 modules also receive good reports.

Cheap and expensive memory

Avoid generic "white-box" memory modules. Such modules are of unknown provenance, and often use memory chips that failed testing by reputable manufacturers or were pulled from rejected modules. Using generic memory is likely to cause stability and data corruption problems. At the other extreme, we also generally avoid the so-called "premium" or "performance" memory modules popular among overclockers. They sell at a substantial premium over standard modules, and seldom provide much real increase in system performance.

For updated recommendations, visit *http://www.hardwareguys.com/picks/memory.html.*

Floppy Drive

Intel and Microsoft have been trying to convince everyone for years that floppy disk drives are "legacy" devices that don't belong in modern PCs. They may even be right. Certainly, we often build PCs without FDDs nowadays. We sometimes regret the lack of an FDD, though, most recently when we built a system around an Intel D845GEBV2 motherboard with a Serial ATA hard drive.

When we attempted to install Windows 2000 and later Windows XP, we found that Windows doesn't recognize S-ATA drives natively on an 845-based motherboard (it does work fine on an 865-series or later). No problem, we thought. We simply restarted Windows 2000 Setup, and at the prompt pressed F6 to tell Windows we had a third-party driver disk. Later, Setup prompted us to insert the driver floppy. We did so, and heard it thunk as it dropped to the bottom of the floppy drive bay. Oops. We'd forgotten that we hadn't installed an FDD in that system.

Faced with either tearing down the system to install an FDD or using another operating system, we put Fedora Linux Disc 1 in the optical drive, rebooted, and watched Linux install without a problem. So much for Window's purported advantages in ease of installation.

But we digress. If you want a floppy disk drive in your system—and installing one is cheap insurance at $8 or so—we recommend using anything at all. FDDs are commodity items, and the brand name makes little or no difference. Recently, we've used 1.44 MB FDDs made by Teac, Toshiba, Sony, IBM, NEC, Mitsumi, and probably some others we've forgotten. In a modern system, an FDD is likely to be used for only a few minutes over the life of the system to install driver updates and BIOS upgrades, so it doesn't matter much what you install.

A combo FDD and card reader

If your case is short on external drive bays, you may face a conundrum. If you install a floppy drive, you have no place to put a card reader; if you install a card reader, you have no place to put a floppy drive. One good solution to this problem is to install a combination FDD/card reader, such as the Mitsumi FA402A (*http://www.mitsumi.com/products/fa402amain.html*).

At $25 or so, the FA402A is an expensive FDD, but it also provides a card reader for CompactFlash, MemoryStick, MicroDrive, MultiMedia Card, Secure Digital Card, and SmartMedia cards. (Olympus/Fujifilm xD-Picture Cards can be used with an adapter.) The FDD portion of the device connects using a standard FDD cable. The card reader connects to an internal USB port. Windows Me, Windows 2000 SP2 or higher, and Windows XP support the card reader natively. Windows 98 SE requires using the provided driver, which you must install *before* you connect the device.

Hard Drive

The good news about choosing a hard disk is that it's easy to choose a good one. Seagate, whose drives we recommend, produces a full range of hard drives at competitive prices. When you buy a hard disk in today's competitive market, you get what you pay for. That said, we prefer Seagate models because we have had reliability problems with drives made by some other manufacturers. Figure 1-8 shows a Seagate Barracuda 7200.7.

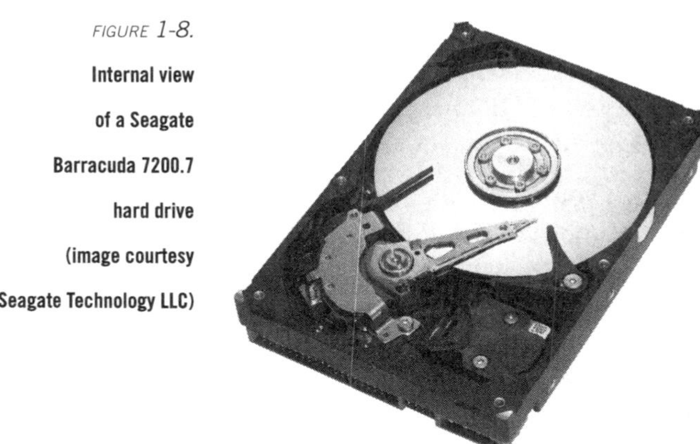

FIGURE 1-8. **Internal view of a Seagate Barracuda 7200.7 hard drive (image courtesy Seagate Technology LLC)**

Manufacturers often have two or more lines of drives that vary in several respects, all of which affect performance and price. Within a given grade of drive, however, drives from different manufacturers are usually closely comparable in features, performance, and price, if not necessarily in reliability. Neither is compatibility an issue, as it occasionally was in the early days of ATA. Any recent ATA hard disk coexists peacefully with any other recent ATA/ATAPI device, regardless of manufacturer. The same is generally true of SCSI drives.

Use the following guidelines when you choose a hard disk:

Choose the correct interface

The first consideration in choosing a hard disk is whether to use standard ATA (Parallel ATA or P-ATA), Serial ATA (S-ATA), or SCSI. P-ATA and S-ATA drives are inexpensive, fast, capacious, and reliable, and are the best choice for most general-purpose systems. SCSI hard drives cost significantly more and require adding an expensive SCSI host adapter, but provide the best performance, particularly under heavy load. Choose your drive interface using the following guidelines:

P-ATA

Choose a P-ATA drive if you are using a motherboard that lacks S-ATA interfaces. Any drive you buy should support UDMA Mode 5 (ATA-100). Only Maxtor produces UDMA Mode 6 (Ultra ATA/133) drives. Ultra ATA/100 has more bandwidth than even the fastest drives require, so Ultra ATA/133 has no real performance advantage. Choose a drive in the size, performance, and price range you want and don't worry about ATA/100 versus ATA/133.

ATA/100 versus ATA/133

A motherboard with ATA/100 interfaces can use ATA/133 drives, and vice versa, but the disk subsystem runs as ATA/100 in either case.

S-ATA

S-ATA drives are generally a bit faster than similar P-ATA models, and use thin cables that improve system cooling relative to wide P-ATA ribbon cables. If your system has S-ATA interfaces and the S-ATA drive you want costs only $5 or $10 more than the P-ATA model, it's worth choosing S-ATA. But if the price differential is much larger, or if you would have to buy a separate S-ATA interface card to use the S-ATA drive, use P-ATA.

SCSI

If disk performance is a major consideration, buy an Ultra320 SCSI host adapter and a 15,000 RPM Ultra320 SCSI drive. Note that you will pay a large premium, both for the drive itself and for the required SCSI host adapter. Purchase a drive and host adapter that comply with the SCAM (SCSI Configured AutoMagically) standard. We recommend and use only Adaptec SCSI host adapters.

Combining SCSI and ATA

When we build a system that requires very high disk performance, we minimize cost when possible by using both SCSI and ATA hard drives. We install a small 15,000 RPM Ultra320 SCSI drive and use it only for data and programs that require its high performance. For bulk storage, we install one or more large ATA drives.

Buy the right size drive

It's tempting to buy the largest drive available, but that's not always the best decision. Very large drives often cost much more per gigabyte than mid-size drives, and the largest drives may have slower mechanisms than mid-size drives. So, in general, decide what performance level you need and are willing to pay for, and then buy a drive that meets those performance requirements, choosing the model based on its cost per gigabyte. All of that said, it may make more sense sometimes to buy the largest drive available despite its high cost per gigabyte and slower performance, simply to conserve drive bays and ATA channels.

Choose a 7,200 RPM drive for a general-purpose system

Hard drives are currently available with rotation speeds that range from 5,400 to 15,000 RPM. All other things being equal, a higher rotation speed provides faster data access and transfer rates, but with correspondingly higher noise and heat.

Nowadays, 5,400 RPM ATA drives are used primarily in "appliance" applications such as set-top boxes, where saving a few bucks in manufacturing cost is a major issue. Some very high capacity ATA drives use 5,400 RPM mechanisms, because these drives are typically used for secondary or "near-line" storage, for which lower performance is an acceptable trade-off for reduced cost. Mainstream ATA drives rotate at 7,200 RPM, and high-performance models at 10,000 RPM. Entry-level SCSI drives rotate at 7,200 RPM, mainstream models at 10,000 or 12,000 RPM, and high-performance models at 15,000 RPM.

We recommend using 7,200 RPM ATA drives for mainstream applications. Choose a 5,400 RPM ATA model only when cost is an overriding concern, and even then you'll save only a few dollars by buying a 5,400 RPM drive rather than a 7,200 RPM unit. Choose a 15,000 RPM SCSI drive only if getting the highest possible disk performance outweighs the significant additional cost.

Get a model with larger buffer/cache if it doesn't cost much more

Disk drives improve performance by buffering reads and writes to a memory cache. Entry-level and mainstream drives typically have a 2 MB cache, and high-performance drives may have 8 MB or more. Some manufacturers sell the same model drive with differing amounts of cache, often indicated by a different letter on the end of the model number. In our experience, larger caches are worth having, but not worth paying much extra for. For example, given two otherwise identical drives, one with 2 MB cache and one with 8 MB cache, we might pay $5 or $10 more for the 8 MB model, but not more. Adding cache is cheap and it does improve performance somewhat, but it doesn't provide the benefits of a fast head mechanism and a fast rotation rate, both of which are more expensive to implement.

Pay attention to noise level and heat production

Few people think about the noise level and heat production of a hard drive, but both are important. A loud hard drive is intrusive, particularly when the heads are seeking. Silence is desirable even in an office setting, but can be critical for such applications as a Home Theater PC. The quietest mainstream hard drives—Seagate Barracuda ATA models—typically idle at about 25dB(A), which is nearly inaudible in a normal environment. Some competing models have idle noise as high as 35dB(A), which is to say they sound literally twice as loud. A cool-running drive is also desirable, because it contributes indirectly to minimizing noise level. The heat produced by a drive must be exhausted from the case, so using a cool drive allows the system fans to run slower (and quieter). The coolest-running mainstream drives are, again, the Seagate Barracuda ATA models.

What to buy

Over the years, we've used hard drives from many manufacturers, including Fujitsu, IBM, Maxtor, Quantum, Samsung, Seagate, Western Digital, and others. All of them have made some excellent drives and some mediocre ones, but over the last few years we've come to use Seagate (*http://www.seagate.com*) drives almost exclusively in our own systems based on their low noise level, high performance, and rock-solid reliability.

Here are the hard drives we recommend.

Any System

Choose a **Seagate Barracuda 7200.8** model of the appropriate size and interface. We use Seagate Barracuda 7200.8 S-ATA drives exclusively in our newer systems. Our older systems use a mix of Seagate Barracuda 7200.7 S-ATA and P-ATA drives.

Recent Seagate S-ATA drives support NCQ (Native Command Queuing), which is similar to the elevator-seeking technology long used by SCSI drives. NCQ drives are faster and more efficient than similar non-NCQ models, particularly under heavy load. NCQ requires a motherboard or add-on PCI S-ATA adapter that provides NCQ-aware S-ATA interfaces, but NCQ drives operate properly (in non-NCQ mode) when connected to an older interface.

Other/special consideration

If you need the faster performance of SCSI, choose a 15,000 RPM Ultra320 SCSI Seagate Cheetah drive and an Adaptec Ultra320 SCSI host adapter. (*http://www.adaptec.com*).

Drive reliability

Drive makers consider drive reliability statistics to be top secret information. It is very difficult for anyone outside the industry to get good data on drive failure rates, but we've done our best. Based on our own considerable experience, reports from readers, and conversations with data-recovery companies, we believe Seagate hard drives to be the most reliable drives available. Accordingly, we recommend Seagate hard drives exclusively.

For updated recommendations, visit *http://www.hardwareguys.com/picks/harddisk.html.*

Optical Drive

Every system needs an optical drive of some sort, if only for loading software. There are several types of optical drives available. Some can use only CDs, which typically store about 700 MB of data. Other optical drives can use DVDs, which typically store about 4,700 MB of data. CD-ROM and DVD-ROM drives are read-only (the "ROM" part of the name). CD writers and DVD writers (also called burners or recorders) can write optical discs as well as read them. DVD is backward compatible with CD, which means that a DVD drive can also read CD discs, and nearly all DVD writers can also write CD discs.

Optical drives range in price from $15 for a basic CD-ROM drive—which only reads CDs—to $150 for a high-end DVD writer, which reads and writes both CDs and DVDs. The price of an optical drive varies according to its capabilities—a DVD drive costs more than a CD drive and a writer costs more than a read-only drive—its brand name, and its speed.

Drive speeds are specified using an "X-factor." The earliest CD-ROM drives transferred data at a constant 150 KB/s, the same rate used by audio CDs, which is referred to as 1X. Later CD drives used variable speeds, changing the speed according to where the head was positioned on the CD. It's impossible to assign a single speed rating to such a drive, so manufacturers began specifying the maximum speed those drives used. For example, a CD-ROM drive that transfers data at a maximum rate 52 times the 150 KB/s audio CD rate, or 7,800 KB/s, is called a 52X Max drive.

DVD drives use the same kind of scheme, but the DVD "X-factor" is different. Rather than the 150 KB/s 1X CD rate, the 1X DVD rate is 1.321 MB/s, or about nine times faster. In other words, a 16X DVD drive transfers data at just over 21 MB/s, nearly three times the rate of a 52X CD drive.

To complicate matters further, optical drives do different tasks at different rates. For example, a typical early CD writer could write CD-R (write-once) discs at 4X, or 600 KB/s, but read discs at 24X, or 3,600 KB/s. When CD-RW (rewritable) discs were introduced, yet a third number was needed, because most CD writers wrote CD-R discs and CD-RW discs at different speeds. A typical modern CD writer might write CD-R discs at 52X, rewrite CD-RW discs at 24X, and read CDs at 52X. Such a drive is referred to as a 52-24-52 drive.

So matters remained, until the first hybrid (or "combo") CD writer and DVD-ROM drive was introduced. At that point, a fourth number was needed to report the DVD-ROM read speed. A typical modern combo drive might write CD-R discs at 52X, rewrite CD-RW discs at 24X, read CDs at 40X, and read DVDs at 16X. Such a drive is referred to as a 52-24-40-16 drive.

But, as the commercial says, just wait, there's more. Along came DVD writers, with not one, not two, but three competing writable DVD formats. We can safely disregard the moribund DVD-RAM standard, but that still leaves DVD-R (and DVD-RW) and DVD+R (and DVD+RW). The DVD-R/RW (so-called "minus") formats seem to be falling behind the DVD+R/RW (so-called "plus") formats, but both—or all four, depending on how you look at it—remain popular. With early DVD writers, you had to pick your format—plus or minus—but most recent DVD writers support both plus and minus discs. All of which they write at different speeds. Arrrghhh.

Although hybrid plus/minus DVD writers cost more than single format plus or minus writers, they are quite popular because people fear choosing a standard that may later be orphaned. Also, it's nice to be able to write to whatever discs happen to be on sale. But it does make it difficult to keep the speeds of various drives straight. The Plextor PX-716A is an excellent example of a modern high-end optical drive. It has the following speeds:

48X (read CD)

48X (write CD-R)

24X (rewrite CD-RW)

16X (read DVD-ROM)

16X (write DVD+R)

8X (rewrite DVD+RW)

16X (write DVD-R)

4X (rewrite DVD-RW)

4X (write dual-layer DVD+R)

So, we could describe the Plextor PX-716A drive as a 48-48-24-16-16-8-16-4-4 model. We could, but we won't, because that way lies insanity.

Choose an optical drive for your system based on the capabilities you need and the price you are willing to pay. Roughly in order of increasing price and usefulness, your choices are:

CD-ROM drive
: When system price is the top priority, using a CD-ROM drive provides the necessary basic functionality at minimum cost. CD-ROM drives read only CD-DA (audio) discs, CD-ROM (data) discs, and (usually) CD-R/CD-RW writable discs. CD-ROM drives are commodity items that sell for as little as $15. Even drives from name-brand Japanese makers such as Sony and NEC sell for $20 or less. In fact, manufacturers make so little profit from CD-ROM drives that they are beginning to disappear from retail channels. The sole advantage of a CD-ROM drive is its low price. The drawbacks of a CD-ROM drive are that it cannot read DVD-Video or DVD-ROM discs and that it cannot write discs. Nearly all current CD-ROM drives read discs at 48X or 52X with similar access times and otherwise similar specifications, so there is little reason to choose a brand other than by price and manufacturer reputation.

DVD-ROM drive
: DVD-ROM drives are also commodities, but cost a bit more than CD-ROM drives—$25 to $35. Like CD-ROM drives, DVD-ROM drives read CD-DA, CD-ROM, and CD-R/RW discs, but also read DVD-Video and DVD-ROM discs. Even for a budget PC, it usually makes sense to spend an extra $10 to get a DVD-ROM drive rather than a CD-ROM drive so the PC can read DVD-Video and DVD-ROM discs. Like CD-ROM drives, DVD-ROM drives are read-only devices, and cannot write discs. Nearly all current DVD-ROM drives read CDs at 40X or 48X and DVDs at 16X with similar access times and otherwise similar specifications, so there is little reason to choose a brand other than by price and manufacturer reputation.

Writable DVD compatibility

If you need a DVD-ROM drive that reads DVD+R/RW and/or DVD-R/RW discs, verify that the model you choose explicitly lists support for the writable DVD formats you need to read. Most current DVD-ROM drives read both "R" (write-once) and "RW" (rewritable) discs in both the "plus" and "minus" formats. Some DVD-ROM drives read "plus" but

not "minus" discs, or vice versa. A few drives, mostly older models, read "R" discs, but not "RW" discs. A few drives, mostly Toshiba models, can also read the moribund DVD-RAM format.

CD-RW drive

CD-RW drives, also called CD writers or CD burners, have also been—you guessed it—largely commoditized. A couple of high-end Plextor models remain available, although for how long is anyone's guess. CD writers read the same formats as CD-ROM drives—CD-DA, CD-ROM, and CD-R/RW discs—but can also write data to inexpensive CD-R (write-once) and CD-RW (rewritable) discs. CD writers typically sell for a bit more than DVD-ROM drives, generally $30 to $40, with high-end Plextor models selling for up to twice that much. Although CD-RW drives do not read DVD discs, they have the inestimable advantage of being able to write discs. In addition to being useful for duping audio and data CDs, CD writers also provide an inexpensive backup solution, albeit limited to about 700 MB per disc. Nearly all current CD-RW drives write CDs at 48X, 52X, or 54X and have similar read speeds, access times, and other specifications, so there is little reason to choose a brand other than by price and manufacturer reputation.

DVD-ROM/CD-RW drive

DVD-ROM/CD-RW "combo" drives combine the functionality of a DVD-ROM drive and a CD-RW drive, and (we're getting tired of saying this...) are largely commoditized. Combo drives sell for a few dollars more than CD writers, typically $45 to $60. Because they can read nearly any optical disc and write CDs, we consider them the best compromise for an inexpensive system. Plextor, alas, discontinued its excellent PlexCombo model.

DVD writer

DVD writers do it all—they both read and write both CDs and DVDs. That flexibility comes at a price, though. Basic DVD writers are available for under $60, but high-end models may cost $150 or more. Here are the issues to consider in choosing a DVD writer:

DVD writable formats supported

Most high-end models can use DVD+R, DVD+RW, DVD-R, and DVD-RW discs interchangeably. A few older models support only DVD+R/RW or only DVD-R/RW. In the past, DVD+R discs cost significantly more than DVD-R discs, and DVD+RW discs significantly more than DVD-RW discs. That price differential has largely disappeared, particularly for name-brand discs. However, it is still possible to buy no-name DVD-R and DVD-RW discs in bulk at a lower price than DVD+R and DVD+RW discs. Although we recommend avoiding cheap discs, if you use a lot of discs for non-critical purposes such as recording TV programs, the lower price of bulk DVD-R/RW media is attractive.

Pluses and minuses

Lower disc prices are the only advantage DVD-R/RW has over DVD+R/RW, and that advantage is disappearing fast. DVD+R/RW is technically superior in every respect to DVD-R/RW. In particular, never use DVD-R/RW discs for backups or other applications where robust error detection and correction is important.

CD writing capabilities

Many people use DVD writers primarily for writing DVDs, and seldom or never write CDs. However, the CD writing features and performance of a drive is important if you frequently use CD-R or CD-RW discs, perhaps to duplicate your audio CDs or for daily backups. If CD writing is important to you, make sure the drive you buy supports at least 32X CD-R writes and, if you use CD-RW, 24X CD-RW rewrites. Also make sure the drive supports BURN-Proof or a similar anti-coaster technology. Ideally, the drive should be Mt. Rainier compliant as well.

Write speed

As is true of CD writers, the write speed of DVD writers becomes pretty much immaterial once you reach a given speed. For us, that speed is 8X. A 4X DVD writer "feels" slow to us. It's not really slow—it's writing data about as fast as a 40X CD writer—but the large capacity of a writable DVD disc means it takes a subjectively "long time," more than 15 minutes, to fill a disc. An 8X DVD writer cuts that time to 8 minutes or so, which feels a lot faster. A 12X DVD writer cuts the time further, to 5 minutes or so, and a 16X writer cuts the time further still, but that small improvement is not nearly as noticeable as the decrease from 15 minutes to 8 minutes. Also, 12X and 16X discs are hard to find and expensive, and that situation is likely to persist for some time. Our advice, therefore, is to buy at least an 8X DVD writer, and to choose a 12X or 16X model only once the price differential has become small.

Blu-Ray and HD-DVD

As we write this in January 2005, high-capacity Blu-Ray and HD-DVD writers are not yet available and drives such as the Plextor PX-716A and NEC ND-3520A that can write dual-layer discs have only recently begun to ship in high volumes. Alas, dual-layer discs are very expensive—literally 10 to 20 times the price of single-layer discs—and are hard to find. So, while it is worth buying a dual-layer capable DVD writer for future flexibility, you may not write many dual-layer discs with it in the near future.

We don't expect Blu-Ray or HD-DVD to have much market presence until late 2005, if then. Only one of these high-capacity formats will be endorsed by the Hollywood studios, which will effectively doom the other to niche status. Discs for current DVD plus and minus writers are likely to remain available for many years, so you needn't fear a drive you buy now being orphaned. For more on the progress of the ongoing DVD format wars, visit *http://www.hardwareguys.com/optical.html.*

What to buy

Here are the optical drives we recommend.

CD-ROM drive

For a CD-ROM drive, your choices are limited and likely to become more so as these drives disappear from the market. We consider any current ATAPI model made by **Lite-On**, **Mitsumi**, **NEC**, **Samsung**, or **Sony** acceptable. All are reliable, so buy on price. Unless the small extra cost is a deal-breaker, we strongly suggest installing a DVD-ROM drive, CD-RW drive, or a hybrid DVD-ROM/CD-RW drive rather than a CD-ROM drive.

CD-RW drive

For a CD-RW drive, look for a 48X, 52X, or 54X model (there is no practical difference in speed) that supports BURN-Proof or some similar "anti-coaster" technology. If you want the most reliable CD-RW drive with the best digital audio extraction (for "ripping" audio CD tracks to your hard drive), choose the **Plextor PlexWriter Premium**, if it is still available. Our second choice is the **Plextor PlexWriter PX-W5224**. Among inexpensive CD writers, we would choose the **Lite-On**

SOHR-5238S or the **Samsung SW-252**, with the **Sony CRX230ED** as runner-up. Otherwise, choose any 48X, 52X, or 54X model from Lite-On, Mitsumi, Samsung, or Sony, based on price.

DVD-ROM drive

For a DVD-ROM drive, choose any current model made by **Lite-On**, **Mitsumi**, **NEC**, **Samsung**, **Sony**, or **Toshiba**. If you need to read writable DVD discs, make sure the model you choose explicitly lists compatibility with the formats you use. If you need to read DVD-RAM discs, buy a Toshiba model. Otherwise, buy on price.

DVD-ROM/CD-RW hybrid drive

We consider a hybrid DVD-ROM/CD-RW drive a good choice for a budget system. For any other system, we recommend using a DVD±R/RW drive instead. If you do decide to use a combination DVD-ROM/CD-RW drive, our first choices are the **Teac DW-552G** and the **Toshiba SD-R1612**, but the **Lite-On SOHC-5232K** and the **Samsung TS-H492A** are also good choices. If you need to read writable DVD discs, make sure the model you choose explicitly lists compatibility with the formats you use. If you need to read DVD-RAM discs, buy the Toshiba SD-R1612. Otherwise, all are reliable and priced similarly, so buy whatever happens to be the least expensive.

DVD±R/RW drive

For a top-quality DVD writer, our first choice is the **Plextor PX-716A**. The **Plextor PX-712A**, the **Sony DRU710A**, and the **Pioneer DVR-A08XL** are also good choices. For those on a tighter budget, our first choice is the **NEC ND-3520A**. It's not a Plextor, but it is a very good drive for the price. We think the **Pioneer DVR-108** and the **Samsung TS-H552B** are a step behind the NEC unit, although they are also good choices. Finally, if you need a competent DVD writer at minimal cost, choose the **Lite-On SOHW-1633S**.

Optical Media

If you care about your data, the blank discs you choose are as important as the drive you use to write them. Here are the discs we recommend:

CD-R: **Taiyo-Yuden** is our first choice. **Maxell**, **TDK**, and **Verbatim** also produce excellent discs.

CD-RW: **Verbatim**

DVD+R: **Taiyo-Yuden**, **Maxell**, or **Verbatim**

DVD+RW: **Taiyo-Yuden** or **Verbatim**

DVD-R: **Use DVD+R instead**, but if you must use DVD-R, use **Maxell**, **TDK**, or **Verbatim** discs.

DVD-RW: **Use DVD+RW instead**, but if you must use DVR-RW, use **Verbatim** discs.

DVD+RW DL: We do not yet have enough experience to recommend a brand of disc.

For updated recommendations, visit *http://www.hardwareguys.com/picks/optical.html.*

Video Adapter

The video adapter, also called a graphics adapter or graphics card, renders video data provided by the processor into a form that the monitor can display. Enthusiast web sites like Tom's Hardware (*http://www.tomshardware.com*) and AnandTech (*http://www.anandtech.com*) spend much of their time testing new graphics adapters and analyzing their 3D gaming performance, but the truth is that 3D performance is unimportant unless you are a gamer.

For the last several years, the video card market has been predictable and boring. Just as Intel and AMD dominate the processor market, ATi and *n*VIDIA dominate the video chipset market. Each has introduced faster and faster AGP video adapters on a roughly yearly product cycle, with each constantly attempting to trump the other's fastest models. There it stood until mid-2004, when Intel introduced the PCI Express (PCIe) interface, which is intended to replace the venerable AGP interface for video adapters.

AGP versus PCI Express

For the time being, PCIe is neither better nor worse than AGP. Both interfaces are more than fast enough to support the fastest current video adapters, so neither has a performance advantage. Physically, the standards are so close that it's difficult to tell at a glance whether you're looking at an AGP or PCIe slot or adapter. Do not hesitate to use AGP for a new system. There is an excellent selection of AGP adapters still available, and AGP adapters will remain available for some time to come. However, AGP is definitely last-generation technology, and will eventually be replaced by PCIe. Currently, the only PCIe motherboards widely available are Pentium 4 models based on Intel 915/925-family chipsets, but Sempron/Athlon 64 motherboards based on *n*VIDIA *n*Force4 chipsets will become increasingly available in 2005.

ATi and *n*VIDIA both scrambled to get new PCIe models to market, and at the same time both were in the midst of rolling out new-generation video chipsets. The result has been a train wreck, with a huge number of cards available based on slightly different chipsets. For example, in January 2005, video adapters were available or announced that used the following chipsets:

ATi

RADEON 7000, 7200, 7500LE, 7500, 8500LE, 8500, 9000, 9000 Pro, 9100, 9100 Pro, 9200SE, 9200, 9200 Pro, 9250, 9500, 9500 Pro, 9550SE, 9550, 9600SE, 9600, 9600 Pro, 9600XT, 9700, 9700 Pro, 9800SE, 9800, 9800 Pro, 9800 XT, X300SE, X300, X600 Pro, X600 XT, X700SE, X700, X700 Pro, X700XT, X800SE, X800, X800 Pro, X800GT, X800XL, X800XT, X800XT Platinum Edition, X850XT, and X850XT PE

nVIDIA

GeForce FX5200LE, FX5200, FX5200U, FX5500, FX5600, FX5600XT, FX5600U, FX5600U LC, FX5700LE, FX5700, FX5700U, FX5700U GDDR3, FX5800, FX5800U, FX5900SE, FX5900, FX5900U, FX5950U, GF6200, GF6600, GF6600GT, GF6800LE, GF6800, GF6800GT, GF6800U, and GF6800U Extreme

Now, certainly, some of those chipsets are obsolescent, and cards based on them range from a $30 ATi RADEON 7000 to a $700+ *n*VIDIA GeForce 6800 Ultra Extreme, but the point is that adapters based on most of these chipsets are available new. In a rational market, ATi and *n*VIDIA might each have five or six chipsets covering the range from $30 video adapters to $600 video adapters, but the video card market is anything but rational right now.

Some chipsets are available only on AGP adapters, others only on PCIe adapters, and still others on both types of adapters. Sometimes the AGP and PCIe versions of an adapter with the same name use different chipsets. Chipsets are announced and disappear almost before products can be built with them. For example, ATi X600-series chipsets had an effective life of only three months between the first shipments and the time they were superseded by the X700-series chipsets.

We were about to say that even we can't keep everything straight, but in fact it's worse than that. Based on conversations with some of our contacts at ATi and *n*VIDIA, we don't think *they* can keep everything straight. So what should you do? We suggest the following:

- Remember that if 3D performance doesn't matter to you, your best option is to choose a motherboard with good embedded video. If embedded video will do the job for you, none of this other stuff matters.

- If you are building a mainstream system for which 3D performance is at least somewhat important, the first decision to make is between AGP and PCIe. In general, AGP motherboards use older technology and are less expensive, while PCIe motherboards offer better upgradability and "future proofing" at a higher price. For most mainstream systems, we think the best course is to choose a $75 to $100 current-generation video adapter without worrying too much about AGP versus PCIe. Chances are you will never replace the original adapter anyway. If you do eventually decide to upgrade, you should be able to find suitable inexpensive adapters in AGP or PCIe without much difficulty.
- For a performance or gaming system, video upgradability is a more important issue, because midrange and high-end AGP adapters will become harder to find as time passes and PCIe becomes dominant. On that basis, PCIe might seem to be the only sensible choice for performance or gaming systems, but unfortunately it is not that simple. If you are building an Intel Pentium 4 system, there's no real question: buy a 915- or 925-based motherboard and a suitable PCIe video adapter. But if you are building an AMD Athlon 64 system, the choice is not as clear. As we write this in January 2005, PCIe Athlon 64 motherboards have just begun shipping in limited quantities, and only premium models are available. Until PCIe Athlon 64 motherboards become more common and affordable, your budget or the features you require may mandate purchasing an AGP Athlon 64 motherboard.
- Once you have decided between AGP and PCIe and set a price range, use the search engines available at online retailers such as NewEgg to determine which adapters are available in your choice of interface and your price range. You may still be faced with a choice among a dozen or two dozen models, but you have at least narrowed down the field significantly. (When we checked NewEgg.com in January 2005, it offered an incredible 787 different video adapters for sale, and that is only a fraction of the total number available.)

Also keep the following in mind when you choose a video adapter:

3D graphics performance is usually not important

We'll say it again: unless you spend most of your computing time running resource-intensive 3D games, performance is the *least* important selection criterion. Don't even consider it. Any current video adapter, and most older models, is more than fast enough to run standard 2D business applications at normal resolutions, such as 1,280 X 1,024.

Previous-generation 3D adapters are discounted deeply when their replacements ship, and are excellent choices for most users. These older video chipsets are often used for embedded video on integrated motherboards, and will suffice for nearly anyone. Don't forget that today's obsolescent chipset was the leading-edge barn burner not long ago. Don't get caught up in the horsepower race, and don't waste money buying performance that you'll never use.

Choose embedded video unless there is good reason not to

Many motherboards sold today provide embedded video at little or no incremental cost over a similar motherboard without video. Pentium 4 motherboards ordinarily provide Intel Extreme Graphics 2 video, which is a part of some Intel chipsets. Some Athlon motherboards provide embedded *n*VIDIA video that is a generation or two behind current standalone *n*VIDIA video adapters. Neither provides high-performance 3D graphics, but either suffices for most purposes, including casual gaming. Unless you need the faster 3D graphics performance or other features (such as TV tuning) available with standalone video adapters, go with the embedded video and spend what you save elsewhere.

Preserve your video options

Make sure any motherboard you buy allows embedded video to be disabled and provides an AGP or PCIe slot. That way, you can upgrade the video later if you need to.

Don't overbuy

If you buy a standalone video adapter, remember that video is just one part of your system. You're likely to be disappointed if you blow your budget on a $400 3D gaming card and make up for that extravagance by settling for a slow processor and inexpensive motherboard. Buy a $150 midrange graphics card instead and spend the other $250 on a faster processor, better motherboard, more memory, and a better display. Video performance will be fast enough for any but the most graphics-intensive games, and overall system performance will be better as well.

Old isn't always bad

If you need better 3D graphics performance than embedded video provides but you don't have much left in the budget for a video adapter, look at "obsolescent" 3D video adapters—those a couple generations out of date. For example, in January 2005 ATi RADEON 7000-series adapters were available for $30 or so. An ATi RADEON

7000 or a similar obsolescent *n*VIDIA adapter can't compare in graphics performance to a current $400 gaming card—or even to a $100 midrange adapter—but for many people it's just the right compromise between cost and performance.

If you buy an older adapter, make sure to verify the level of DirectX it supports. The RADEON 7000, for example, supports DX7. If you plan to play a game that requires DX8 or DX9, the older adapter will be of little benefit. This problem is self-limiting, though. You are unlikely to want to run 3D applications that require a very recent version of DirectX on an older card. Such applications require more graphics power than older cards can provide.

Buy only an AGP 2.0/3.0 or PCI Express x16 video adapter

If you decide to install a standalone video adapter, buy only a 1.5V AGP 4X (AGP 2.0) or 0.8V AGP 4X/8X (AGP 3.0) adapter or an x16 PCIe model. Check the motherboard manual to verify which type or types of adapter it supports, and then buy accordingly. Most current AGP motherboards use either 0.8V AGP 3.0 cards only or 1.5V AGP 2.0 and 0.8V AGP 3.0 cards interchangeably. Fortunately, the PCI Express standard has not yet fragmented, so any PCIe adapter fits any PCIe motherboard.

But old can be dangerous

Some older AGP motherboards have mechanical, electrical, or chipset limitations that prevent them from working properly with some AGP cards. Conversely, some older AGP cards do not function properly in some AGP motherboards. These problems were caused both by ambiguities in the AGP standard and by some manufacturers failing to adhere closely enough to the published standard. These problems were relatively common with motherboards and video adapters designed and sold until late 2000, and in particular with motherboards that use some older VIA chipsets. No current motherboards or AGP cards that we know of suffer these incompatibilities. If you're building your new system using a motherboard or AGP card that you salvaged from an older system, check the maker's web site for details about possible conflicts.

Give more weight to 2D display quality than to 3D performance

Display quality is subjective and very difficult to quantify, but a real issue nonetheless. The three major video chipset companies are ATi and *n*VIDIA, both of which provide chipsets that are used both for standalone AGP adapters and for embedded video, and Intel, whose Extreme Graphics 2 is available only as embedded video.

ATi

ATi produces a wide range of video chipsets. 3D performance ranges from moderate in the least expensive models to extremely high in the most expensive models. 2D video quality is excellent across the entire line and at any resolution. ATi drivers balance 3D performance and 2D image quality, favoring neither at the expense of the other.

nVIDIA

*n*VIDIA produces a wide range of video chipsets. 3D performance ranges from moderate in the least expensive models to extremely high in the most expensive models. 2D video quality ranges from mediocre in older models, particularly high-performance versions, to very good in some later models. We generally consider *n*VIDIA 2D image quality acceptable at low resolutions, but less so at 1280 X 1024 and higher. *n*VIDIA drivers tend to favor 3D performance at the expense of 2D image quality.

Intel

Intel Extreme Graphics 2 video is built into some Intel chipsets, and is available only in embedded form. 3D performance is at best moderate, although it is acceptable for casual gaming. 2D display quality is very good to excellent.

Make sure drivers are available for your operating system

Make sure that the adapter you choose has drivers available for the operating system you intend to use. This is particularly important if you run Linux or another OS with limited driver support. The best vendors, like *n*VIDIA, provide frequent driver updates for a broad range of operating systems and versions. Consider the manufacturer's history of providing frequent driver updates and supporting new operating system versions, which you can determine by examining the manufacturer's web site, checking the newsgroups, and cruising the hardware enthusiast web sites.

Linux video drivers

Video driver availability may be an important consideration for Linux users. Most recent Linux distributions have basic 2D support for most popular video adapters, but may lack support for 3D acceleration, TV, dual-head, and other features. In the past, many Linux users chose Matrox for their excellent Linux support, but now *n*VIDIA is generally acknowledged to have the best Linux support. Although ATI ignored Linux for years, excellent 2D and (less excellent) 3D drivers are now available for ATI RADEON 8500 and later adapters, as well as some earlier models. Before you choose a video adapter for a Linux system, check the maker's web site and *http://x.org* to determine if acceptable drivers are available. You may also want to check the Linux distribution you are considering to make sure that the installer will detect and configure hardware 3D support without much hassle.

If you buy a high-performance video card, make sure it has a good warranty

Video cards used to be among the most reliable components of a PC. This is changing, not because manufacturers are cutting corners, but because new high-performance video cards are pushing hardware technology to the limit. Having a video card die after only six months or a year is now relatively common, particularly for those who push the card past its limit by overclocking it in pursuit of the highest possible performance. We've seen video cards with 90-day warranties, which is completely unacceptable. Regard one year as an absolute minimum, and longer is better.

Make sure the video adapter provides the interface(s) you need

Most analog CRT monitors use the familiar high-density DB15 "VGA" connector, although a few high-end models also support RGB component video. Flat panel displays (FPDs) use a variety of connectors, including the analog DB15VGA connector (typically used by low-end FPDs), or one of three different types of Digital Visual Interface (DVI) connectors. Midrange and higher FPDs normally provide a DVI-D digital connector, and may also provide a DB-15 analog connector and/or a DVI-A analog connector. If you want to run dual FPDs, make sure the video adapter you choose has dual DVI connectors.

Video adapters and FPDs

If you plan to use an FPD, whenever possible choose an FPD and a video adapter that both provide DVI-D connectors. FPD image quality is hit-or-miss if you use an analog connection, because video data originates in digital form, is converted to analog by the video adapter, and is then converted back to digital by the FPD. These multiple AD/DA conversions can introduce various artifacts, none of which is pleasing. Also, some analog video adapters simply don't "play nice" with some FPDs, and there's enough variation from one sample to another that about the only way to know for sure it to try it. This problem seems to be worse with DB-15 analog connections than with DVI-A connections, but the only sure way to avoid it is to use a digital path end-to-end.

What to buy

Here are the video adapters we recommend.

Economy or Business System

For a general-purpose economy or business/corporate system, choose embedded video. We prefer ATi or Intel embedded video, but nVIDIA is also acceptable. Make sure the motherboard you select has an AGP 3.0 or PCIe slot so that you can upgrade the video later if necessary.

Mainstream System

For a mainstream system, choose a $75 to $100 AGP or PCIe video adapter. Our first choice is the **ATi X300 (PCIe)** or **ATi RADEON 9600 (AGP)**, but the ***n*VIDIA 6200** (PCIe) is also a good choice. *n*VIDIA 5200-series AGP adapters are slower, but also acceptable.

ATi/DirectX versus nVida/Open GL

Across the board, *n*VIDIA models typically outperform ATi models in OpenGL games, sometimes dramatically, whereas ATi models often outperform similarly-priced *n*VIDIA models in DirectX games. If you spend much time playing recent 3D games, choose accordingly.

Performance or Gaming System

For a performance or gaming system, 3D performance matters. The best budget choice is the **ATi X700 (PCIe)** or **ATi RADEON 9600 XT** (AGP), but the ***n*VIDIA 6600 (PCIe/AGP)** is an acceptable second choice. For a mainstream 3D graphics adapter, the ***n*VIDIA 6600 GT**

(PCIe/AGP) is the standout choice, but the **ATi X700 XT** and the **ATi X700 Pro** are also reasonable selections. For a premium 3D graphics adapter, our first choice is the ***n*VIDIA 6800GT**, although the **ATi X800 XT** (PCIe) and **ATi X800 Pro** (AGP) are also good choices. If only the best will do, and your budget runs to a $500+ video adapter, the best choice is the ***n*VIDIA 6800 Ultra Extreme**, if you can find one for sale. The standard ***n*VIDIA 6800 Ultra** costs a bit less and is a bit slower, but is still wickedly fast. The **ATi X800 XT Platinum Edition** (PCIe/AGP) is priced like the 6800 Ultra Extreme and slower than the standard 6800 Ultra, but is a good choice if you prefer ATi video adapters.

Linux System
: Unfortunately, neither *n*VIDIA nor ATi provides open-source drivers for their video adapters. Both do, however, provide propriety binary Linux drivers. Although ATi has begun to catch up, *n*VIDIA binary Linux drivers have historically been faster and more full-featured than ATi drivers. There is still a noticeable gap, and so we recommend using an nVIDIA adapter if you run Linux, and particularly if you run 3D games under Linux.

For updated recommendations, visit *http://www.hardwareguys.com/picks/video.htm*

Display

The first decision to make when you choose a display is whether to go with a traditional "glass bottle" CRT monitor or an LCD flat-panel display (FPD).

CRT monitors versus FPDs

Relative to CRT monitors, flat-panel displays have the following advantages:

Brightness
: FPDs are on average brighter than CRTs. A typical CRT might have brightness of about 100 candelas/square meter, a unit of measurement referred to as a *nit*. (Some monitors are rated in foot Lamberts (fL), where one fL equals about 3.43 nits.) A high-quality 15" FPD might be rated at 300 nits, three times as bright as a typical CRT. This brightness disparity decreases a bit in larger sizes. For example, a high-quality 19" FPD might be rated at 235 nits. CRTs dim as they age, although a brightness control with enough range at the upper end can often be used to set an old CRT to near original brightness. The *cold cathode ray tubes (CCRTs)* used to backlight FPDs also dim as they age, but generally fail completely before reduced brightness becomes a major issue.

Contrast

Contrast measures the difference in luminance between the brightest and dimmest portions of an image, and is expressed as a ratio. The ability to display a high-contrast image is an important aspect of image quality, particularly for text. An average CRT monitor may have a contrast ratio of 200:1, and a superb CRT 250:1. An inexpensive FPD may have a contrast ratio of 200:1, and a superb FPD 500:1. In other words, even an inexpensive FPD may have a better contrast ratio than an excellent CRT monitor.

Usability in bright environments

Even good flat-screen CRTs are subject to objectionable reflections when used in bright environments, such as having the screen facing a window. Good FPDs are much superior in this respect. Short of direct sunlight impinging on the screen, a good FPD provides excellent images under any lighting conditions.

Size and weight

A typical CRT is at least as deep as its nominal screen size. For example, a 17" CRT is often 17" or more from front to back. Large CRTs may be difficult to fit physically in the available space. Conversely, FPDs are quite shallow. The panel itself typically ranges from 1.5" to 3" deep, and even with the base most FPDs are no more than 7" to 8" deep. Also, where a large CRT may weigh 50 to 100 pounds or more, even large FPDs are quite light. A typical 15" FPD might weigh 12 pounds, a 17" unit 15 pounds, and even a 20" unit may weigh less than 25 pounds. That small size and weight means that it's possible to desk- or wall-mount an FPD with relatively inexpensive mounting hardware, compared to the large, heavy, expensive mounting hardware needed for CRTs.

CRT versus FPD screen sizes

Stated FPD display sizes are accurate. For example, a 15" FPD has a display area that actually measures 15" diagonally. CRT sizes, on the other hand, are nominal because they specify the diagonal measurement of the entire CRT, part of which is covered by the bezel. For example, a nominal 17" CRT might have a display area that actually measures 16" diagonally. A couple of lawsuits several years ago convinced CRT makers to begin stating the usable size of their monitors. This is stated as *VIS* (*viewable image size* or *visible image size*), and is invariably an inch or so smaller than the nominal size.

This VIS issue has given rise to the belief that a 15" FPD is equivalent to a 17" CRT, a 17" FPD to a 19" CRT, and so on. In fact, that's not true. The image size of a typical 17" CRT is an inch or so larger than that of a 15" FPD, as is the image size of a 19" CRT relative to a 17: FPD.

Power consumption

A typical 17" or 19" CRT consumes 100 to 125 watts while operating. A typical 15" FPD consumes 35 watts, a typical 17" FPD 50 watts, and a typical 19" FPD 70 watts. At 20% to 60% the power consumption of a typical CRT, FPDs reduce electricity bills directly by consuming less power, and indirectly by reducing heating loads on air conditioning systems.

Flat-panel displays also have many drawbacks relative to CRT monitors. Note that not all FPDs suffer from all of these flaws, that newer models are less likely than older models to suffer from any particular flaw, and that inexpensive models are much more likely than premium models to suffer from these flaws, both in number and in degree.

Cost

The primary downside of flat-panel displays is their hideously high cost. For example, for the $300 cost of a good entry-level 15" FPD, you could buy *two* good 17" CRT monitors or one superb 19" CRT monitor, either of which provides both a larger display area and better display quality than the entry-level FPD. This is one area in which newer, better FPD models suffer much more than older, less capable models, because a good new FPD isn't cheap.

Fixed resolution

FPDs are designed to operate at exactly one resolution, which is nearly always 1024 X 768 for a 14" or 15" FPD and 1280 X 1024 for a 17", 18", or 19" FPD. Although you *can* run an FPD at lower resolution than it was designed to use, you don't want to. At non-native resolution, your choices are to have a sharp image that occupies only a portion of the FPD screen, or to use pixel extrapolation, which results in a full-screen image, but with significantly degraded image quality.

Backlight failure

A typical FPD uses an array of four cold cathode ray tubes (CCRTs), which are similar to fluorescent tubes and provide the backlight without which the image cannot be seen. In early FPDs, the CCRTs were often rated at as little as 10,000 hours of life. That sounds like a long time until you realize that if you leave such a display on 24 hours a day, the rated lifetime of the tubes is only about 417 days. And, of course, components do sometimes fail before their rated lifetime has expired, and the presence of four tubes quadruples the likelihood of an early failure. The upshot was that early FPDs were often warranted for three years, but with only a one-year warranty on the CCRTs. Many people found that these early models failed within that one-year period or shortly thereafter. That was disastrous, because early 17" FPDs cost $2,000 or more and could not be repaired. Instead, for all practical purposes, they had to be remanufactured at a cost that was typically half to two-thirds the cost of a new display.

The situation is somewhat better with recent model FPDs. Most manufacturers now use upgraded CCRTs that are rated for at least 25,000 hours, and better models use CCRTs rated for 50,000 hours. Also, although some current FPD models have been redesigned to allow the CCRTs to be replaced without remanufacturing the entire unit, replacing a backlight properly is a finicky job, even for the manufacturer. Accordingly, nearly all FDP manufacturers replace the entire unit rather than attempting to replace the CCRTs. However the job is done, replacing the CCRTs out of warranty is an expensive repair, even assuming that replacement parts are still available when your unit needs to be repaired. Be very conscious of the rated CCRT lifetime and warranty terms for any FPD you buy. Look for at least a three-year warranty that covers parts and labor on all components, specifically including the CCRTs.

Poor display of fast motion video

Unlike phosphor pixels, which can be turned on or off almost instantly, transistorized FPD pixels have a rise time and fall time which may be noticeable when the screen displays fast-action video. On inexpensive FPDs, this may be noticeable as a "smearing" effect during operations as undemanding as dragging a window to another location. More expensive FPD units deal with this problem better, but even the best of the current FPD units are not fast enough to deal well with demanding fast-motion video such as 3D gaming.

Limited viewing angle

CRTs present essentially the same image quality regardless of viewing angle. Conversely, FPDs present their best image quality only within a relatively small viewing angle, although better FPD units have larger viewing angles. When comparing viewing angles, make sure you're comparing apples to apples. Some manufacturers specify total angles, whereas other specify only half-angles from the perpendicular. For example, one manufacturer might specify a viewing angle of 80 degrees above and below the centerline, while another might specify a total angle of 120 degrees. The first display, of course, has a total viewing angle of 160 degrees—80 above and 80 below the centerline—which is 40 degrees greater than the second display, but that may not be clear. Note that some FPDs specify different horizontal and vertical viewing angles.

Color shifting

Most graphic artists we've spoken to refuse to use FPDs, because the appearance of colors and the relationship between colors change depending on the viewing angle. This problem is particularly acute with inexpensive FPDs, although even premium units exhibit it at least to some extent. The newest, most expensive FPD models minimize this problem to the extent that most people will not notice it, but those who insist on accurate color reproduction will likely still prefer high-end CRT monitors.

Pixel defects

An FPD panel is manufactured as a monolithic item that contains on the close order of one million pixels. Even though current manufacturing processes are quite good, many FPD panels have one or a few defective pixels. These defective pixels may be always-on (white), always-off (black), or some color. People vary in their reaction to defective pixels. Many people won't even notice a few defective pixels, while others, once they notice a defective pixel, seem to be drawn to that pixel to the exclusion of everything else. Most manufacturer warranties specifically exclude some number of defective pixels, typically between five and ten, although the number may vary with display size and, sometimes, with the location of the defective pixels and how closely they are clustered. As long as the display meets those requirements, the manufacturer considers the display to be acceptable. You may or may not find it acceptable.

Image persistence

Image persistence causes an image that has been displayed for a long time to remain as a ghost-like second image, similar to the burn-in problem on old monochrome monitors. This effect, although it is not permanent, can be quite disconcerting, particularly if you are working with images rather than text. This problem is much more common with older and inexpensive FPDs than with high-end current models.

Flat color rendering

Although the contrast and brightness of recent high-end FPDs are excellent, most FPDs provide subjectively less vibrant color than a good CRT monitor. This is particularly evident in the darkest and lightest ranges, where the tones seem to be compressed, which limits subtle gradations between light tones or dark tones that are readily evident on a good CRT. Also, many FPDs seem to add a color cast to what should be neutral light or dark tones. For example, dark neutral tones may appear shifted toward the blue (cooler) or red (warmer) ranges. Again, this problem is less prevalent in high-quality, expensive FPDs than in entry-level units, and is also more likely to occur if you are using an analog interface versus a digital interface.

Our opinion is that FPDs should be used only if their size, weight, low power consumption, or portability outweigh their much higher cost and other disadvantages. Otherwise, we recommend you choose a good CRT and allocate the money you save by going with a CRT to other system components.

Choosing a CRT monitor

Use the following guidelines when choosing a CRT monitor:

- Remember that a monitor is a long-term purchase. Even with heavy use, a high-quality monitor can be expected to last five years or more, whereas inexpensive monitors may fail within a year or two.
- Make sure the monitor is big enough, but not too big. Verify that your desk or workstation furniture can accommodate the new monitor. Many people have excitedly carried home a new 19" or 21" monitor only to find that it literally won't fit where it needs to. Check physical dimensions and weight carefully before you buy. Large monitors commonly weigh 50 lbs. or more, and some exceed 100 lbs. That said, if you find yourself debating between buying one monitor and another that's the next size up, go with the larger monitor. But note that if your decision is between a low-end larger monitor and a high-end smaller one for about the same price, you may well be happier with the smaller monitor. A $150 17" monitor beats a $150 19" monitor every time.
- Avoid reduced-depth monitors whenever possible. Space constraints may force you to choose a short-neck model. Just be aware that you will pay more for such a monitor, and its image quality will be lower.
- Stick with good name brands and buy a midrange or higher model from within that name brand. That doesn't guarantee that you'll get a good monitor, but it does greatly increase your chances. The monitor market is extremely competitive. If two similar models differ greatly in price, the cheaper one likely has significantly worse specs. If the specs

appear similar, the maker of the cheaper model has cut corners somewhere, whether in component quality, construction quality, or warranty policies.

The best brands

Deciding which are the "good" name brands is a matter of spirited debate. Our opinion, which is shared by many, is that until their departure from the CRT market Sony and Hitachi made the best CRT monitors available, although they sold at a premium. We now consider NEC-Mitsubishi, Samsung, and ViewSonic to be the "Big Three" monitor makers. Most of their monitors, particularly midrange and better models, provide excellent image quality and are quite reliable. Many people also think highly of EIZO/Nanao monitors. You're likely to be happy with a monitor from any of these manufacturers, although we confess that we now buy only NEC-Mitsubishi monitors for our own primary systems.

Further down the ladder are "value" brands like Mag Innovision, Princeton, Optiquest, and others. Our own experience with value brands, albeit limited, has not been good. A Princeton monitor we bought died a month out of warranty, as did an OEM Mag Innovision model that we bought bundled with a PC. Two Mag Innovision monitors developed severe problems after only a year or two of use. In our experience, which covers many hundreds of monitors purchased by employers and clients, the display quality of the value brand monitors is mediocre, and they tend not to last long.

- If possible, test the exact monitor you plan to buy (not a floor sample) before you buy it. If you have a notebook computer, install DisplayMate on it (the demo version is adequate and can be downloaded from *http://www.displaymate.com/demos.html*) and use it to test the monitor. If you don't have a notebook, take a copy of DisplayMate with you to the store and get permission to run it on one of their machines. In return for the higher price you're paying, ask the local store to endorse the manufacturer's warranty—that is, to agree that if the monitor fails you can bring it back to the store for a replacement rather than dealing with the hassles of returning the monitor to the manufacturer. Mass merchandisers like Best Buy usually won't do this (they try to sell you a service contract instead, which you shouldn't buy), but small local computer stores may agree to endorse the manufacturer's warranty. If the monitor has hidden damage from rough handling during shipping, that damage will ordinarily be apparent within a month or two of use, if not immediately.

Buy CRT monitors locally

Buy the monitor locally if possible. After shipping costs, it may actually cost less to buy locally, but that is not the main reason for doing so. Buying locally gives you the opportunity to examine the exact monitor you are buying. Monitors vary more between examples than other computer components. Also, monitors are sometimes damaged in shipping, often without any external evidence on the monitor itself or even the box. Damaged monitors may arrive DOA, but more frequently they have been jolted severely enough to cause display problems and perhaps reduced service life, but not complete failure. Buying locally allows you to eliminate a "dud" before you buy it, rather than having to deal with shipping it back to the vendor or manufacturer.

- Most mainstream monitor manufacturers produce no 15" models (there's no profit in them), and usually three—Good, Better, and Best—models in 17", 19", and 21". In general, the Good model from a first-tier maker corresponds roughly in features, specifications, and price to the Better or Best models from lower-tier makers. For casual use, choose a Good model from a first-tier maker, most of which are very good indeed. If you make heavier demands on your monitor—such as sitting in front of it 8 hours a day—you may find that the Better model from a first-tier maker is the best choice. The Best models from first-tier makers are usually overkill, although they may be necessary if you use the monitor for CAD/CAM or other demanding tasks. Best models often have generally useless features like extremely high resolutions and unnecessarily high refresh rates at moderate resolutions. It's nice that a Best 17" model can display 1600 X 1200 resolution, for example, but unless you can float on thermals and dive on rabbits from a mile in the air, that resolution is likely to be unusable. Similarly, a 17" monitor that supports 115 MHz refresh rates at 1024 X 768 is nice, but in practical terms offers no real advantage over one that supports 85 or 90 MHz refresh.
- Decide which makes and models to consider (but not the specific unit you buy) based on specifications. Any monitor you consider should provide at least the following:

Controls

Power; Degauss (if not automatic); Contrast; Brightness; Horizontal Size; Horizontal Position; Vertical Size; Vertical Position; Pincushion/Barrel Distortion Adjustment. Better monitors may add some or all of the following: On-Screen Display; Focus; Individual Red, Green, Blue Color Control (or Color Temperature); Tilt; Align; and Rotate.

Warranty

Inexpensive monitors often have a one-year parts and labor warranty (although 90-day warranties, particularly on labor, are not unheard of). Better monitors usually warrant the tube for two or three years (often excluding labor after the first year) with one-year parts and labor on the remaining components. Warranties on high-quality monitors may be for three years parts and labor. In reality, the value of a long warranty on a good monitor is less than it might seem. The few times we've seen a good monitor fail, it's either been soon after it was taken out of the box or after many years of use. Conversely, a two- or three-year warranty on an inexpensive monitor would be useful indeed, because such monitors frequently fail after a couple of years. That's why you seldom find a good, long, comprehensive warranty on a cheap monitor.

Other specifications vary according to monitor size. Remember that shadow mask dot pitches are not directly comparable with aperture grill stripe pitches. A 0.28 mm diagonal dot pitch corresponds roughly to a 0.25 mm stripe pitch. Also, not all dot pitches are specified in the same manner. Some manufacturers specify the diagonal dot pitch. Others specify individual horizontal dot pitch and vertical dot pitch. A monitor specified as having a 0.22 mm horizontal dot pitch and 0.13/0.15 mm vertical dot pitch corresponds roughly to a monitor with a 0.27 mm diagonal dot pitch. The minimum specifications are listed, with preferable values in parentheses:

15"

13.8" viewable image size (VIS); flat-square tube (FST); 0.28 mm diagonal dot pitch; maximum resolution 1024 X 768 (1280 X 1024); 75 Hz (85 Hz) refresh rate for standard 800 X 600 resolution. Automatically synchronize at 31 to 69 KHz (31 – 80 KHz) horizontally and 55 to 120 Hz (50 – 130 Hz) vertically.

17"

15.6" (15.8") VIS; FST; 0.28 mm (0.27 mm) diagonal dot pitch; maximum resolution 1280 X 1024 (1600 X 1200); 85 Hz (100 Hz) refresh rate for standard 1024 X 768 resolution, and 75 Hz

(85 Hz) refresh rate at 1280 X 1024. Automatically synchronize at 31 to 69 KHz (31 – 95 KHz) horizontally and 55 to 120 Hz (50 – 160 Hz) vertically.

19"

17.8" (18.0") VIS; FST; 0.28 mm (0.27 mm) diagonal dot pitch; maximum resolution 1600 X 1200 (1920 X 1440); 85 Hz (100 Hz) refresh rate for standard 1280 X 1024 resolution, and 75 Hz (85 Hz) refresh rate at 1600 X 1200. Automatically synchronize at 31 to 94 KHz (31 – 110 KHz) horizontally and 55 to 160 Hz (50 – 160 Hz) vertically.

21"

19.8" (20.0") VIS; FST; 0.28 mm (0.27 mm) diagonal dot pitch; maximum resolution 1600 X 1200 (2048 X 1536); 85 Hz (100 Hz) refresh rate for standard 1600 X 1200 resolution, and 75 Hz (85 Hz) refresh rate at resolutions above 1600 X 1200. Automatically synchronize at 31 to 96 KHz (31 – 125 KHz) horizontally and 55 to 160 Hz (50 – 160 Hz) vertically.

- Choose the specific monitor you buy based on how it looks to you. Comparing specifications helps narrow the list of candidates, but nothing substitutes for actually looking at the image displayed by the monitor. For example, monitors with Sony Trinitron tubes have one or two fine horizontal internal wires whose shadows appear on screen. Most people don't even notice the shadows, but some find them intolerable.
- Make sure the monitor has sufficient reserve brightness. Monitors dim as they age, and one of the most common flaws in new monitors, particularly those from second- and third-tier manufacturers, is inadequate brightness. A monitor that is barely bright enough when new may dim enough to become unusable after a year or two. A new monitor should provide a good image with the brightness set no higher than 50%.

Like all other component manufacturers, monitor makers have come under increasing margin pressures. A few years ago, we felt safe in recommending any monitor from a first-tier maker, because those companies refused to put their names on anything but top-notch products. Alas, first-tier makers have been forced to make manufacturing cost reductions and other compromises to compete with cheap Pacific Rim monitors.

Accordingly, low-end models from first-tier makers may be of lower quality than they were in the past. The presence of a first-tier maker's name plate still means that monitor is likely to be of higher quality than a similar no-name monitor, but is no longer a guarantee of top quality. Many first-tier monitors are actually made in the same Pacific Rim plants that also produce no-name junk, but don't read too much into that. First-tier monitors are still differentiated by component quality and the level of quality control they undergo. There is no question in our minds that the first-tier monitors are easily worth the 10% to 20% price premium they command relative to lesser brands. In fact, we think it is worth the extra cost to buy not just a first-tier monitor, but a midrange first-tier monitor. We prefer NEC Mitsubishi models, including their entry-level models, but the midrange and better Samsung and ViewSonic models are also excellent.

Choosing an FPD

If you have weighed the trade-offs carefully and decided that an FPD is right for you, use the following guidelines when choosing a flat-panel display:

- Current FPDs are available in analog-only, digital-only, and hybrid analog/digital models. Analog input is acceptable on 15" models running 1024 X 768, but on 17" models running 1280 X 1024 analog video noise becomes an issue. At that level of resolution, analog noise isn't immediately obvious to most users, but if you use the display for long periods the difference between using a display with a clean digital signal and one with a noisy analog signal will affect you on almost a subconscious level. At 1024 X 768, we regard an analog signal as acceptable. At 1280 X 1024, we regard a digital signal as very desirable but not essential for most users. Above 1280 X 1024, we regard digital signaling as essential.

- Insist on full 24-bit color support. Most current FPDs support true 24-bit color, allocating one full byte to each of the three primary colors, which allows 256 shades of each color and a total of 16.7 million colors to be displayed. Many early FPDs and some inexpensive current models support only 6 bits per color, for a total of 18-bit color. These models use extrapolation to simulate full 24-bit color support, which results in poor color quality. If a monitor is advertised as "24-bit compatible," that's probably good reason to look elsewhere. Bizarrely, many FPDs that do support true 24-bit color don't bother to mention it in their spec sheets, while many that support only 18-bit color trumpet the fact that they are "24-bit compatible."

- Most FPD makers produce two or three series of FPDs. Entry-level models are often analog-only and use standard thin film transistor (TFT) panels. Midrange models usually accept analog or digital inputs, and may use enhanced TFT panels. Professional models may be analog/ digital hybrids or digital-only, and use enhanced TFT panels with IPS (In-Plane Switching) or MDVA (Multi-Domain Vertical Alignment). Choose an entry-level TFT model only if you are certain that you will never use the display for anything more than word processing, web browsing, and similarly undemanding tasks. If you need a true CRT-replacement display, choose a midrange or higher enhanced TFT model. For the highest possible image quality, choose a high-end model that supports IPS and is made by a top-tier manufacturer.

- Decide what panel size and resolution is right for you. Keep in mind that when you choose a specific FPD model, you are also effectively choosing the resolution that you will always use on that display.
- Verify the rated CCRT life. For an entry-level FPD that will not be used heavily, a 25,000 hour CCRT life is marginally acceptable. If you will use the FPD heavily, insist on CCRTs rated at 50,000 hours.
- Buy the FPD locally if possible. Whether or not you buy locally, insist on a no-questions-asked return policy. FPDs are more variable than CRT monitors, both in terms of unit-to-unit variation and in terms of usability with a particular graphics adapter. This is particularly important if you are using an analog interface. Some analog FPDs simply don't play nice with some analog graphics adapters. Also, FPDs vary from unit to unit in how many defective pixels they have and where those are located. You might prefer a unit with five defective pixels near the edges and corners rather than a unit with only one or two defective pixels located near the center of the screen.
- In return for the higher price you pay at a local store, ask them to endorse the manufacturer's warranty—that is, to agree that if the FPD fails you can bring it back to the store for a replacement rather than dealing with the hassles of returning the FPD to the manufacturer.
- If possible, test the exact FPD you plan to buy (not a floor sample) before you buy it. Ideally, in particular if you will use the analog interface, you should test the FPD with your own system, or at least with a system that has a graphics adapter identical to the one you plan to use. We'd go to some extremes to do this, including carrying our desktop system down to the local store. But if that isn't possible for some reason, still insist on seeing the actual FPD you plan to buy running. That way, you can at least determine if there are defective pixels in locations that bother you.

- Decide which models to consider (but not the specific unit you buy) based on specifications. Any FPD you consider should provide at least the following:

  Controls
  : Auto adjust, brightness, contrast, horizontal position, vertical position, phase, clock, color temperature, RGB color adjustments, saturation, hue, recall default settings, and save custom settings.

  Warranty
  : Inexpensive FPDs may have a one-year parts and labor warranty, which is inadequate. Inexpensive models may instead have a three-year warranty on parts and labor, but warrant the CCRTs for only one year. In effect, that's just a one-year warranty with window dressing, because the CCRTs are the one component that is by far the most likely to fail. Insist on a three-year parts and labor warranty that covers all parts, including CCRTs. If the manufacturer offers an extended warranty that covers all parts, consider buying that warranty.

Other specifications vary according to FPD size. For 15" models, the minimum specifications for an analog FPD are listed with preferable values for an analog/digital FPD in parentheses. For 17" and larger models, although analog-only models are available, we do not recommend those and so list only minimum specifications for a digital FPD:

15"
: TFT flat panel; 15-pin VGA analog connector (15-pin analog, DVI-D, S-video, and RGB composite connectors); pixel pitch, 0.297 mm; contrast ratio, 300:1 (500:1); brightness, 200 nit typical (300 nit typical); maximum resolution 1024 X 768 at 60 Hz or 75 Hz for analog (1024 X 768 at 60 Hz or 75 Hz at 60 Hz or 75 Hz for analog and 1024 X 768 at 60 Hz for digital); viewing angle 120° horizontal by 85° vertical (130° by 110°); autosync range 31.5 to 60 KHz horizontal and 56 to 75 Hz vertical; video clock frequency 80 MHz; rise time 40 ms (25 ms); fall time 40 ms (25 ms).

17" and larger
: TFT flat panel; DVI-D connector; pixel pitch, 0.264 mm; contrast ratio, 400:1; brightness, 250 nit typical; maximum resolution 1280 X 1024 at 60 Hz digital; viewing angle 150° horizontal by 140° vertical; autosync range 24 to 80 KHz horizontal and 56 to 75 Hz vertical; video clock frequency 135 MHz; rise time 25 ms; fall time 25ms.

- Choose the specific FPD you buy based on how it looks to you. Comparing specifications helps narrow the list of candidates, but nothing substitutes for actually looking at the image displayed by the FPD. Some people like all FPDs, some dislike all FPDs, and some have strong preferences for one or another brand of FPD.

In flat-panel displays, the best choices are more limited than for CRT monitors. Until recently, we considered the first tier in flat-panel displays to include only Hitachi and Fujitsu, with Samsung straddling the low first-tier/high second-tier boundary. Alas, Hitachi departed the FPD market in August 2004, and Fujitsu FPDs are not widely distributed. Fortunately, first-tier CRT makers have improved their FPD product lines, and we now consider FPDs from NEC, Samsung, Sony, and ViewSonic worthy of consideration.

What to buy

Here are the displays we recommend.

15" CRT

We do not recommend buying any 15" CRT monitor. A 17" model costs only a few dollars more and provides much more display area. If for some reason you must have a 15" CRT monitor, choose the **NEC AS500** (*http://www.necmitsubishi.com*) or the **ViewSonic E55** (*http://www.viewsonic.com*). The ViewSonic E50 is a few dollars cheaper and a bit less desirable.

17" CRT

If you're on a tight budget, our first choice is the **NEC AS700**, although the **ViewSonic E70** is also a good choice. For a mainstream monitor, we think the **ViewSonic G75F+B** is the best choice, with the **NEC FE770/FE771** or the **Samsung 793DF** our second choices, and the **NEC AS750** or the **ViewSonic G70** our third choices.

Do not buy a premium 17" CRT monitor. Although high-end 17" monitors are available, we see no point to paying $175 or more for a 17" monitor. For little more than the cost of a premium 17" monitor, you can instead buy an entry-level 19" monitor from a first-tier maker. That 19" monitor supports the same or higher resolutions as the premium 17" monitor. The image scale at those resolutions will actually be large enough to use, and the image quality of the entry-level 19" will be more than good enough for general use.

19" CRT

For a budget 19" CRT, our first choice is the **NEC AS900**, with the **ViewSonic E90** not far behind. For a mainstream 19" CRT, choose the **NEC FE991**, although the **Samsung 997DF** and the **ViewSonic P95F** are also excellent monitors. We can't make a recommendation for a premium 19" CRT because we've never used one. The mainstream models are more than good enough for anything other than specialized high-resolution work such as CAD/CAM or medical imaging.

Like most people, we have less experience with FPDs than with CRT monitors. However, we have generally come to favor Samsung and Sony models based on the image quality of units we have seen. Here are the models we recommend:

15" FPD

We do not recommend any budget 15" FPD. Those we have seen have poor display quality and questionable reliability. For a mainstream 15" model, choose the **NEC ASLCD51V** or **ViewSonic VG500**, both of which are excellent. We think it makes little sense to buy a premium 15" FPD—good 17" models cost little more—but the best premium 15" FPD we know of is the **Sony SDM-X53**. The **Samsung 510N** and the **ViewSonic VG510** are also excellent premium 15" models.

17" FPD

For a budget 17" FPD, our first choice is the **Samsung 710N**, although the **ViewSonic VX715** and **NEC ASLCD71VM** are also good choices. For a mainstream 17" FPD, our first choice is the **Sony SDM-S74** or **Sony SDM-X73**, with the **NEC LCD1760V** coming in second and the **ViewSonic VG710** third. For a premium 17" FPD, the standout choice is the **Samsung 173P**, with the **NEC LCD1760NX**, **Samsung 172X**, **Samsung 710T**, and **ViewSonic VP171** sharing second place.

19" FPD

For a budget 19" FPD, our first choice is the **Samsung 910T**, with the **ViewSonic VG900** in second place. For a mainstream 19" FPD, our first choice is the **Sony SDM-S94** or **Sony SDM-X93**, with the **NEC LCD1915X** in second place. For a premium 19" FPD, the **Samsung 193P** is the best choice, with the **NEC LCD1980SX** or the **ViewSonic VP912** a good second choice.

20"+ FPD

Although they have only one extra inch of diagonal size, 20" and larger FPDs run at 1600 X 1200 resolution rather than the 1280 X 1024 resolution used by 19" FPDs. We have little knowledge of 20" FPDs, so we can make no recommendations. However, several of our colleagues have tested large FPDs, so we will pass along their advice. Our friend Jerry Pournelle tested the 20" **LaCie photon20visionII** and raves about its display quality. He liked it so much, in fact, that he decided to buy the review sample LaCie sent him rather than returning it after the evaluation period expired. Several of our colleagues, including at least one graphic artist, have also recommended the **Hewlett-Packard L2035** 20" FPD.

FPDs and Linux

As odd as it sounds, some FPDs are not compatible with Linux. This is true because some FPDs do not provide physical buttons or knobs to configure the display. Instead, you must use a Windows-only utility to change settings for the display. If you currently use Linux or think there's any chance you'll do so in the future, avoid such models.

For updated recommendations, visit *http://www.hardwareguys.com/picks/displays.html.*

Audio Adapter

Audio adapters, also called sound cards, are a dying breed. Nearly all motherboards provide embedded audio that is more than good enough for most people's needs. In particular, the embedded audio provided by *n*VIDIA and Intel chipsets is excellent, with good support for six or more audio channels. Only gamers, those who work professionally with audio, and those who have purchased a motherboard without embedded audio need consider buying a standalone audio adapter.

Gaming and embedded audio

Gamers dislike embedded audio not so much because it lacks features or sound quality but because embedded audio puts a small burden on the main system processor, which can reduce graphics frame rates slightly. Also, the best gaming audio adapters, such as the Sound Blaster Audigy 2 ZS Platinum Pro include features that appeal primarily to gamers.

What to buy

We won't presume to advise audio professionals, but for others who need a standalone audio adapter here are the ones we recommend.

Economy, Business, Mainstream, or SFF System

For economy, business/corporate, mainstream, and small form factor (SFF) systems—indeed for nearly any system—embedded audio more than suffices. The best embedded audio by far is *n*VIDIA SoundStorm audio, but alas *n*VIDIA has dropped SoundStorm from their recent chipsets because of licensing costs. The best embedded audio available with current-generation chipsets is Intel High-Definition (HD) Audio, available with Intel 9XX-series chipsets, but even the basic embedded audio provided by nearly all recent and current chipsets is perfectly adequate for most purposes.

Performance System

Performance systems deserve better audio than is available with embedded audio chipsets, and the **M-Audio Revolution 7.1** (*http://www.m-audio.com*) is by far the best choice in general-purpose standalone audio adapters. The Revolution 7.1 strikes a good balance. It has excellent sound quality, not far behind the aging but still superb Turtle Beach Santa Cruz, and gaming support second only to the Sound Blaster Audigy 2 LS adapters, which unfortunately have relatively poor sound quality for general use. Our second choice is the **M-Audio Revolution 5.1** and our third choice is the venerable **Turtle Beach Santa Cruz** (*http://www.turtlebeach.com*). We award the Santa Cruz third place only because its gaming support is somewhat inferior to that of the M-Audio cards and substantially inferior to that of the Sound Blaster Audigy 2 LS cards. If you do not use your performance system for gaming, the Santa Cruz should be your first choice.

Newer isn't always better

Turtle Beach recently introduced two new audio adapters in 2004. The Catalina is their performance sound card. It sells for about $70 and is targeted at gamers. The Riviera is their new entry-level audio sound card. It sells for $40 or so, and is targeted at people who have older motherboards with unsatisfactory embedded audio and want to upgrade to better audio at low cost. Although we expected great things from these new cards based on our experience with the Santa Cruz, we were disappointed. We cannot recommend either of these adapters.

Gaming System

Creative Labs Sound Blaster cards (*http://www.soundblaster.com*) own the gaming market, and for good reason. They provide the best feature sets for gaming and enjoy the broadest support from game software makers of any sound card on the market. Unfortunately, although their feature sets, particularly their support for the latest version of Creative's EAX audio standard, are an excellent fit for gamers, their overall sound quality is not up to the best available from other consumer-grade sound cards from M-Audio and Turtle Beach. That means you have to make a trade-off between gaming support and sound quality, so choose a sound card for your gaming system with that in mind.

For a budget gaming system, embedded audio may suffice, depending on the games you play and your expectations for audio support. If you need a budget standalone gaming sound adapter, we think the **Sound Blaster Audigy LS** is the best choice. If you're willing to give up some gaming support for better general sound quality, the **M-Audio Revolution 5.1** is an excellent choice, and the **Turtle Beach Santa Cruz** provides even better sound quality at the expense of still less gaming support.

For a mainstream gaming system, the best choice is the **Sound Blaster Audigy 2 ZS**, although the **M-Audio Revolution 7.1** has many advocates. For a dedicated high-end gaming system, there's no real choice. Go with the **Sound Blaster Audigy 2 ZS Platinum Pro**.

Linux System

If you run Linux, the situation is a bit more complicated. We have had few problems configuring embedded or standalone audio adapters under Linux, but we attribute most of that success to our chosen distro, Xandros. In each case, we simply install the ALSA drivers, reboot the system, and everything just works. Several of our colleagues, however, point out that embedded audio is problematic with many Linux distributions, and we do dimly recall sometimes tearing our hair out trying to get embedded audio working under several Linux distros before we changed over to Xandros.

Linux sound drivers typically support fewer features than Windows drivers. For example, Linux drivers may not support hardware acceleration for a particular sound card, or may support only two-channel stereo output on a 5.1 or 7.1 channel card. Linux is a very poor gaming platform anyway, so it makes sense to disregard gaming support and choose a sound card based solely on audio quality. Our colleagues point out, and our experience confirms, that the best choice for audio under Linux is the **Turtle Beach Santa Cruz**. We've been using Santa Cruz cards for years now, and have used them with many Linux distros with nary a problem. Although our experience with them under Linux is limited, the **M-Audio Revolution 7.1/5.1** cards are well supported by the ALSA (free) drivers and the OSS (commercial) drivers and seem to be relatively trouble-free.

Speakers

Computer speakers span the range from $10 pairs of small satellites to $500+ sets of six or seven speakers that are appropriate for a home theater system. As is true of displays and input devices, personal preference is the most important factor in choosing speakers.

Speakers that render a Bach concerto superbly are often not the best choice for playing a first-person shooter like Unreal Tournament. For that matter, speakers that one person considers perfect for the Bach concerto (or the UT game), another person may consider mediocre at best. For that reason, we strongly suggest that you attempt to listen to speakers before you buy them, particularly if you're buying an expensive set.

Speaker sets are designated by the total number of satellite speakers, followed by a period and a "1" if the set includes a subwoofer (also referred to as a low-frequency emitter or LFE). For example, a speaker set that includes only two satellites is called a 2.0 speaker set. One that adds a subwoofer is called a 2.1 speaker set. A 4.1 speaker set has four satellites—left and right, front and rear—and a subwoofer. A 5.1 speaker set adds a center-channel speaker, which is useful primarily for watching movies on DVD. A 6.1 speaker set adds a rear center-channel speaker, which is primarily of interest to gamers.

The price of a speaker set doesn't necessarily correspond to the number of speakers in the set. For example, there are very inexpensive 5.1 speaker sets available, and some 2.0 sets that cost a bundle. We recommend that you decide on the number of speakers according to your budget. If you have $75 to spend, for example, you're much better off buying a decent 2.1 speaker set than a cheesy 5.1 speaker set.

What to buy

As a starting point, and subject to what your own ears tell you, here are the speaker sets we recommend.

2.0

For a budget 2.0 speaker set, our first choice is the **Creative Labs SBS270** (*http://www.creative.com*). The **Creative Labs SBS250** or the **Logitech X-120** (*http://www.logitech.com*) cost a few dollars less and are sufficient for listening to music and casual gaming, as is our third choice, the **Altec-Lansing 200** (*http://www.altec-lansing.com*). The sound quality of any of these speaker sets is surprisingly good for the price, much better than no-name 2.0 speaker sets that sell for under $10. For a mainstream 2.0 speaker set, our first choice is the **JBL Duet** (*http://www.jbl.com*) and our second choice is the **Altec-Lansing MX5020**. For a premium 2.0 speaker set, our first choice is the **M-Audio StudioPro 4** (*http://www.m-audio.com*), although the **M-Audio Studiophile DX4** is also an excellent set. For a super-premium 2.0 speaker set, the Swans M200 (*http://www.swanspeaker.com*) are unbelievably good, as they should be for nearly $200.

2.1

For a budget set, our first choice is the **Logitech X-230**, with the **Altec-Lansing VS2121** not far behind. The **Creative SBS330**, **Labtec Pulse 485** (*http://www.labtec.com*), and **Altec-Lansing 121** are also good budget sets. For a mainstream set, we prefer the **Logitech Z-3e/i**, although the **Altec-Lansing VS4121**, **Creative I-Trigue 3300/3350**, and **Logitech Z3** are also good choices. For a premium set, the **Klipsch GMX A-2.1** (*http://www.klipsch.com*) is the standout choice, with the **Creative I-Trigue 3500** and **Klipsch ProMedia 2.1** good second choices. We'd put the **Altec-Lansing MX5021/FX6021** in third place in this category.

4.1

There aren't many choices in 4.1 sets, because most manufacturers focus on 2.1 and 5.1 sets instead. For a budget 4.1 set, we'd go with the **Creative SBS450**. For a mainstream set, the best option is the **Logitech Z-560**.

5.1

For a budget 5.1 set, our first choices are the **Logitech Z-640** and the **Logitech X-530**, with the **Altec-Lansing VS3151** and **Creative Inspire P5800** sets a step behind. Our third choices in this category are the **Creative Inspire P5400** and the **Creative SBS560**. For a mainstream 5.1 set, we prefer the **Logitech Z-5300**, with the **Creative Inspire GD580** our second choice. For a premium 5.1 set, you can't go wrong with the **Klipsch ProMedia Ultra 5.1** or the **Logitech Z-5500**. The **Creative GigaWorks S700** and the **Logitech Z-680** are also excellent choices in this price range.

6.1

Choices in 6.1 (and 7.1) sets are limited, again because manufacturers focus on 2.1 and 5.1 sets. For a budget 6.1 set, we recommend the **Logitech X-620**. For a mainstream set, choose the **Creative MegaWorks 650**.

7.1

For a budget 7.1 set, choose the **Creative Inspire T7700** or the **Creative Inspire P7800**. We know of no 7.1 sets in what we consider the mainstream price range. For a premium 7.1 set, choose the **Creative GigaWorks S750**.

Keyboard

The ancient Romans had good advice for choosing a keyboard—*"de gustibus non est disputandum"*—loosely translated, "it's useless to argue about matters of personal preference." A keyboard we really like, you may dislike intensely, and vice versa. Ultimately, your own preferences are the best guide.

Keyboards vary both in obvious ways—layout, size, and form—and in subtle ways like key spacing, angle, dishing, travel, pressure required, and tactile feedback. People's sensitivity to these differences varies. Some are keyboard agnostics who can sit down in front of a new keyboard and, regardless of layout or tactile response, be up to speed in a few minutes. Others have strong preferences about layout and feel. If you've never met a keyboard you didn't like, you can disregard these issues and choose a keyboard based on other factors. If love and hate are words you apply to keyboards, use an identical keyboard for at least an hour before you buy one for yourself.

That said, here are several important characteristics to consider when you choose a keyboard:

Choose the proper physical style

Keyboards are available in two major physical styles, the older-style "straight" keyboard and the modern "ergonomic" style. Some people strongly prefer one or the other style. Barbara, for example, hates ergonomic keyboards, which she refers to as "melted" or "deformed." Robert, on the other hand, doesn't care much which style he uses. He has an ergonomic keyboard on his primary office desktop system and several secondary systems, but a straight keyboard on his system in the den, which he uses heavily in the evening. If you've never used an ergonomic keyboard, give one a try before you buy your next keyboard. You may hate it—everyone does at first—but then again after you use it for an hour or so you may decide you love it.

Consider layout

The position of the primary alphanumeric keys is standard on all keyboards other than those that use the oddball Dvorak layout. What varies, sometimes dramatically, is the placement, size, and shape of other keys, such as the shift keys (Shift, Ctrl, and Alt), the function keys (which may be arrayed across the top, down the left side, or both), and the cursor control and numeric keypad keys. If you are used to a particular layout, purchasing a keyboard with a similar layout makes it much easier to adapt to the new keyboard.

Choose the USB interface
Most current keyboards use the USB interface natively, and are supplied with an adapter for those who need to connect them to a PS/2 keyboard port.

Make sure your operating system supports extended keyboard functions
Some keyboards provide dedicated and/or programmable function keys to automate such things as firing up your browser or email client or to allow you to define custom macros that can be invoked with a single keystroke. These functions are typically not built into the keyboard itself, but require loading a driver. To take advantage of those functions, make sure a driver is available for the OS you use.

Programmable keyboards and Linux

If you run Linux or another non-Windows operating system, avoid programmable keyboards that require drivers—as most do—unless those drivers are available for your chosen operating system. Instead, choose a programmable keyboard that stores and executes macros itself. Such keyboards are uncommon nowadays, and cost more than standard keyboards. The best locally-programmable keyboards we know of are the CVT Avant Stellar and Avant Prime models (*http://cvtinc.com*).

Consider weight
Although it sounds trivial, the weight of a keyboard can be a significant issue for some people. The lightest keyboard we've seen weighed just over a pound, and the heaviest was nearly eight pounds. If your keyboard stays on your desktop, a heavy keyboard is less likely to slide around. Conversely, a very heavy keyboard may be uncomfortable for someone who works with the keyboard in his lap.

Avoid multi-function keyboards
Keyboards are low-margin products. As a means to differentiate their products and increase margins, some manufacturers produce keyboards with speakers, scanners, and other entirely unrelated functions built in.

These functions are often clumsy to use, fragile, and have limited features. If you want speakers or a scanner, buy speakers or a scanner. Don't get a keyboard with them built in.

Consider a wireless keyboard for special purposes

Various manufacturers make wireless keyboards, which are ideal for presentations and TV-based web browsing. Wireless keyboards include a separate receiver module that connects to a USB port or the PS/2 keyboard port on the PC. The keyboard and receiver communicate using either radio frequency (RF) or infrared (IR). IR keyboards require direct line-of-sight between the keyboard and receiver, while RF keyboards do not. Most IR keyboards and many RF keyboards provide very limited range—as little as five feet or so, which limits their utility to working around a desk without cables tangling. Some RF keyboards and a few IR keyboards use higher power to provide longer range, up to fifty feet or more. These are often quite expensive and provide relatively short battery life. Whichever type of wireless keyboard you get, make sure it uses standard (AA/AAA/9V) alkaline or NiMH batteries rather than a proprietary NiCd battery pack, which is subject to the infamous NiCd memory effect whereby NiCd batteries soon begin to lose the ability to hold a charge.

Son of Northgate OmniKey

The Northgate OmniKey keyboard, with its function keys down the left and a satisfyingly clacky feel, has attained nearly cult status among some users, although Northgate itself is long gone. Original OmniKey keyboards haven't been produced for years, so remaining working examples are sought after like Old Masters. Fortunately, there's an alternative. Creative Vision Technologies, Inc. (*http://www.cvtinc.com*) makes the Avant Stellar keyboard, which is more or less a clone of the Northgate OmniKey Plus. It isn't cheap, but it's as close as you'll find to the OmniKey in a current keyboard.

What to buy

Logitech and Microsoft both produce a wide range of excellent keyboards, one of which is almost certainly right for you. Even their basic models are well-built and reliable. The more expensive models add features such as RF or Bluetooth wireless connectivity, programmable function keys, and so on.

We used Microsoft keyboards almost exclusively for many years, and continue to recommend them. However, when we tested several Logitech keyboards some months ago, we found that we actually preferred their features and feel. We currently use Logitech keyboards on many of our primary systems, although we also use various Microsoft keyboards, both older and current models, on several systems.

Avoid inexpensive, no-name keyboards.

For updated recommendations, visit *http://www.hardwareguys.com/picks/keyboards.html*.

Mouse

Choosing a mouse is much like choosing a keyboard. Personal preference is by far the most important consideration. Before you buy a mouse, look for an opportunity to try out the model you are considering.

Use the following guidelines when choosing a mouse:

Get the right size and shape

Mice are available in various sizes and shapes, including very small mice intended for children, notebook-sized mice, the formerly-standard "Dove bar" size, the mainstream ergonomic mouse, and some very large mice that have many buttons and extra features. Most people find nearly any standard-size mouse comfortable to use for short periods, but if you use a mouse for extended periods small differences in size and shape often make a big difference in comfort and usability. Although oversize mice like the Microsoft IntelliMouse Explorer provide attractive features and functions, people with very small hands often find such mice too large to use comfortably. Pay particular attention to mouse shape if you are left-handed. Although Microsoft claims that their asymmetric ergonomic mice are equally usable by left- and right-handers, many lefties find them uncomfortable and so resort to right-handed mousing. Other manufacturers, including Logitech, produce symmetric mice for which chirality is not an issue.

Small hand, big mouse?

Don't assume that hand size and mouse size are necessarily related. For example, Barbara, who has small hands, prefers the Microsoft IntelliMouse Explorer, which is an oversized mouse. She found that using a standard or small mouse for long periods caused her hand to hurt. Changing to a large mouse solved the problem.

Get a wheel mouse

Although some applications do not support the wheel, those that do are the ones most people are likely to use a great deal—Microsoft Office, Internet Explorer, Mozilla, and so on. Using the wheel greatly improves mouse functionality by reducing the amount of mouse movement needed to navigate web pages and documents.

Consider a mouse with extra buttons

Standard two-button mice (three, counting the wheel) are adequate for most purposes. However, five-button mice are ideally suited to some applications, such as games and web browsing. For example, the two extra buttons can be mapped to the Back and Forward browser icons, eliminating a great deal of extraneous mouse movement. Recent Microsoft mice provide a tilting scroll wheel. Rotating the wheel moves you up or down in the document; tilting the wheel from side to side scrolls horizontally.

Make sure the cord is long enough

We have seen mice with cords ranging in length from less than 4 feet to about 9 feet. A short mouse cord may be too short to reach the system, particularly if it is on the floor. If you need a longer mouse cord, purchase a PS/2 keyboard extension cable, available in nearly any computer store.

Consider a cordless model

If your desktop is usually cluttered, consider buying a cordless mouse. The absence of a cord can make a surprising difference.

Buy an optical mouse

Old-style optical mice were a pain in the begonia. They required special mousing surfaces with fine embedded wires and frequently malfunctioned. The new generation of optical mice introduced by Microsoft several years ago—what we call "red-eye mice"—changed that. They use a red LED light source and do not require any special mousing surface. We have used them on such featureless surfaces as a beige computer case and a plain sheet of paper. Basically, they work fine with anything other than a mirror or similarly reflective surface.

Because they are sealed units, red-eye mice do not require the frequent cleaning that mechanical mice do. Robert had to take his mechanical mice apart and clean them literally every few days, but red-eye mice can go for months at a time without any cleaning other than a quick wipe with a damp cloth. Good red-eye mice are very precise and extremely durable. Robert's den system had a Microsoft red-eye mouse, which he dropped to the hardwood floor several times a week. Finally, after more than two years of this abuse, the red-eye mouse died with a horrible rattle. The replacement—a Logitech optical mouse—continues to work perfectly, despite frequent falls.

Try a trackball

Trackballs have never really caught on, probably because most require using the thumb to move the pointer. At least one newer model, the red-eye Microsoft Trackball Explorer, resembles a mouse and allows using the index finger to point. In our experience, about 1 of every 10 people who try a trackball becomes a trackball convert. But trackballs sell probably only 1% the volume of mice, which says there are a lot of people who don't know what they're missing. Trackballs are also available in red-eye versions, and we prefer those to the mechanical versions for ease of maintenance.

What to buy

Logitech and Microsoft both produce a wide range of excellent optical mice, in corded and cordless models. One of them is almost certainly right for you. Even their basic models are well-built and reliable. The more expensive models have more features, are more precise, and are probably more durable.

We used Microsoft optical mice almost exclusively for many years, and continue to recommend them. However, when we tested the superb Logitech MX-series optical mice, we found that we preferred their shape and feel. We now use Logitech optical mice on many of our primary systems, although we also use various Microsoft optical mice, both older and current models, on several systems.

Avoid inexpensive, no-name mice. If someone attempts to sell you a mechanical "ball" mouse, run away.

For updated recommendations, visit *http://www.hardwareguys.com/picks/mice.html.*

Network Adapter

A network adapter—also called a LAN (Local Area Network) adapter, or NIC (Network Interface Card)—is used to connect a PC to a home or business network. A network adapter provides a relatively fast communication link—from 10 megabits per second (Mb/s) to 1,000 Mb/s—between the PC and other devices connected to the network. Network adapters are available in wired and wireless versions. A network may use all wired network adapters, all wireless network adapters, or some combination of the two.

Wired network adapters

In a typical wired network, the network adapters in each PC connect to a central hub or switch that allows any connected device to communicate with any other connected device. In a home or SOHO setting, a wired network adapter may also be used to connect an individual PC directly to a cable modem or xDSL modem.

Nearly all wired network adapters support one or more of a family of networking standards that are collectively called Ethernet. Early Ethernet adapters connected to thick coaxial cable (10Base5) or thin coaxial cable (10Base2), and communicated at 10 Mb/s. More recent Ethernet adapters use unshielded twisted pair (UTP) cable, which resembles standard telephone cable, and communicate at 10 Mb/s (10BaseT), 100 Mb/s (100BaseT or "Fast Ethernet"), or 1,000 Mb/s (1000BaseT or "Gigabit"). All wired Ethernet adapters use an 8-position, 8-connector (8P8C) jack that resembles an oversized telephone jack, and is usually (although incorrectly) called an "RJ-45" connector.

LAN adapter compatibility

Most Ethernet adapters are backward-compatible with slower Ethernet versions. For example, most 100BaseT adapters can also communicate with 10BaseT devices, and most 1000BaseT adapters can also communicate with 100BaseT and 10BaseT devices. This is not invariably true, however. Some Ethernet devices support only one or two standards. That can cause problems if, for example, you connect a 10BaseT adapter to a hub or switch that supports only 100BaseT or 100BaseT and 1000BaseT. Although the devices can be physically connected, they do not communicate. Components that support multiple speeds, called hybrid components, are usually labeled in the form 10/100BaseT, 100/1000BaseT, or 10/100/1000BaseT.

Many motherboards include embedded wired Ethernet adapters, which are typically 10/100 or 10/100/1000 hybrid devices. You can add wired Ethernet to a system that lacks an embedded NIC by installing an inexpensive PCI expansion card.

Embedded network adapters are reliable and add little or nothing to the cost of a motherboard, but they do extract a small performance penalty because they generally use the main system CPU for some processing tasks.

Standalone desktop PCI network adapters typically cost from $15 to $40, depending on manufacturer and speed. (Adapters intended for servers cost more, sometimes much more.) PCI network adapters place little or no load on the main system CPU, and are often more efficient and fully-featured than embedded adapters.

The best rule of thumb for most desktop systems is to use an embedded network adapter, if your chosen motherboard offers that option and if you do not require the additional management and other features available only with standalone adapters. For servers, use a standalone 100BaseT PCI network adapter, unless you are using a special server motherboard that incorporates one or more server-class 100BaseT or 1000BaseT network adapters. For 1000BaseT on a server, use only an embedded or PCI Express adapter. A PCI 1000BaseT adapter simply consumes too much of the available PCI bandwidth to be usable in such an environment.

Networking over phone lines

One oddball form of wired networking deserves brief mention. The Home Phoneline Networking Alliance (HPNA) defines a set of standards that allow data to be transferred on existing telephone cables within a business or residence. HPNA transmits digital data at high frequencies using the spare bandwidth of the telephone cables, which means network transmissions do not interfere with normal use of the telephone line for voice, fax, or dial-up modem use, nor does voice and other analog traffic interfere with network transmission quality.

The initial HPNA 1.0 specification, released in late 1998, essentially overlaid standard Ethernet protocols on analog telephone lines, but had a maximum data rate of only 1 Mb/s. HPNA 2.0, released a year later, boosted the transmission rate to 10 Mb/s, the same as 10BaseT Ethernet. Although many companies produced internal PCI HPNA adapters and external USB HPNA adapters, they were relatively expensive and finicky. Accordingly, HPNA never caught on as a mainstream technology, and was relegated to niche status at best.

The impetus behind HPNA was to provide an easy, inexpensive solution for situations in which running an Ethernet cable was difficult or expensive. When HPNA was introduced, 802.11* wireless networking was slow, expensive, and unreliable. Now that 802.11* wireless networking is fast, inexpensive, and reliable, HPNA is obsolete.

Wireless network adapters

Wireless network adapters—also called WLAN (wireless LAN) cards or 802.11 cards—use radio waves to communicate. WLAN adapters communicate with a central device called an access point (AP) or wireless access point (WAP). In a mixed wired/wireless network, the AP connects to the wired network and provides an interface between the wired and wireless portions of the network. One AP can support many WLAN adapters, but all of the adapters must share the bandwidth available on the AP. In a large network, multiple APs may be used to extend the physical reach of the wireless network and to provide additional bandwidth to computers that connect to the network with WLAN adapters.

WLAN adapters are commonly used in notebook computers, and may be built-in or added via a Cardbus adapter. WLAN adapters are also available as PCI expansion cards that can be installed in desktop systems. These provide a useful alternative when it is difficult or expensive to run a cable to a system. For example, although the rest of our home network uses wired 100BaseT and 1000BaseT components, we installed a WLAN adapter in our Home Theater PC system because it resides near an exterior wall and there was no convenient way to run an Ethernet cable to it.

The original 1997-era WLAN adapters used a standard called 802.11, which supported a maximum data rate of only 2 Mb/s. Those adapters are long obsolete. Current WLAN adapters support one or more of the following standards.

802.11b

The 802.11b specification was released in mid-1999, and devices based upon it soon flooded the market. 802.11b supports a maximum data rate of 11 Mb/s, comparable to 10BaseT Ethernet, and has typical real-world throughput of about 5 Mb/s. 802.11b uses the unlicensed 2.4 GHz spectrum, which means it is subject to interference from microwave ovens, cordless phones, and other devices that share the unlicensed 2.4 GHz spectrum. The popularity of 802.11b is waning because components that use faster standards, described later, are now available at a reasonable cost. Millions of 802.11b adapters remain in use, primarily as embedded or PC Card adapters in notebook computers.

802.11a

Most people think that 802.11a is a more recent standard than 802.11b because 802.11a is significantly faster than 802.11b and because 802.11a components did not arrive on the market until a year or more after 802.11b components were widely available. In fact, the IEEE released the 802.11a and 802.11b standards at the same time. 802.11a was slower to catch on because it originally required an FCC license and because 802.11a components were significantly more expensive than comparable 802.11b components.

802.11a supports a maximum data rate of 54 Mb/s, and has typical real-world throughput of about 25 Mb/s. It uses a portion of the 5 GHz spectrum that was formerly licensed, which limited interference from other devices. Unlike the wild-and-wooly 2.4 GHz spectrum, where anyone at all could play without permission, the 5 GHz spectrum was tightly regulated to avoid interference. Although that portion of the spectrum is now unlicensed, it remains relatively uncluttered. The real downside of 802.11a is that the laws of physics dictate that a 5 GHz signal has shorter range and is more easily obstructed than a 2.4 GHz signal. Also, because 802.11a uses the 5 GHz spectrum, it is incompatible with 802.11b.

The higher cost and mandatory licensing for 802.11a devices meant that until recently, when the license requirement was removed, they were used almost exclusively in business environments. 802.11a components also typically have business-oriented features such as remote manageability that increase costs and are of little interest to home users. However, 802.11a, which for a time seemed moribund, is seeing a renaissance that is primarily driven by home users who have found that the 5 GHz spectrum used by 802.11a is much more reliable for such tasks as streaming video wirelessly.

802.11g

The most recent WLAN standard is 802.11g, which combines the best features of 802.11a and 802.11b. Like 802.11b, 802.11g works in the 2.4 GHz spectrum, which means it has good range but is subject to interference from other 2.4 GHz devices. Because they use the same frequencies, 802.11b WLAN adapters can communicate with 802.11g APs, and vice versa. Like 802.11a, 802.11g supports a maximum data rate of 54 Mb/s, and has typical real-world bandwidth of about 25 Mb/s. In the absence of interference, that is sufficient to support real-time streaming video, which 802.11b cannot.

802.11g components did not sell well at first because they cost much more than similar 802.11b components. That is no longer the case. 802.11g components now sell for only a few dollars more than their 802.11b analogs, and so 802.11g has for all intents and purposes made 802.11b obsolete.

802.11 brand (in)compatibility

In theory, 802.11b and 802.11g components are standards-based, so components from different manufacturers should interoperate. In practice, that is largely true, although minor differences in how standards are implemented can cause conflicts. In particular, some high-end 802.11b/802.11g components include proprietary extensions for security, faster performance, and similar purposes. Those components do generally interoperate with components from other vendors, but only on a "least common denominator" basis—that is, using only the standard 802.11 features. In general, the best way to ensure that your wireless network operates with minimal problems is to use WLAN adapters and APs from the same vendor.

"802.108g"

Several manufacturers, including D-Link and NetGear, produce APs that claim to provide 108 Mb/s bandwidth. In fact they do, but only by "cheating" on the 802.11g specification. Such APs, colloquially called "802.108g" devices, work as advertised, but using them may cause conflicts with 802.11g-compliant devices operating in the same vicinity.

The problem is this: 802.11g defines 11 channels (13 in Europe), each with 22 MHz of bandwidth. Each 22 MHz channel can support the full 54 Mb/s bandwidth of 802.11g. But these channels overlap, as shown in Figure 1-9. Three of the channels—1, 6, and 11—are completely non-overlapping, which means that three 802.11g-compliant APs in the same vicinity—one assigned to each of the three non-overlapping channels—can share the 2.4 GHz spectrum without conflicts. Alternatively, two 802.11g-compliant APs can be assigned to two channels that do not overlap each other, for example, Channels 2 and 8.

Unfortunately, the design of 802.108g devices is such that they claim not just 2/3 of the available spectrum, but all of it. Rather than use the top 2/3 or the bottom 2/3 of the range, current 802.108g devices use the middle 2/3, leaving only small spectrum segments at either end of the range unused. Because the spectrum segments left unused by 802.108g are not a full channel wide, no other 2.4 GHz 802.11 devices can operate in the vicinity of an 802.108g device that is operating in full-speed 108 Mb/s mode.

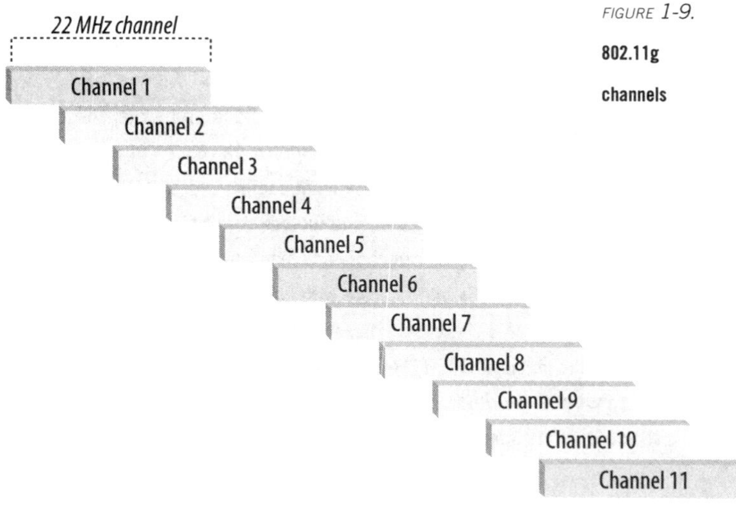

FIGURE 1-9. **802.11g channels**

Someone may be listening

If you use wireless networking, keep in mind that you are broadcasting your data omni-directionally. The range of 802.11b/g is up to several hundred feet with a normal antenna, and can be extended to several miles by using a simple antenna built from a soup or potato chip can. In fact, rumor has it that U.S. surveillance satellites can easily receive 802.11b/g broadcasts from orbit.

Unless you enable encryption, which is usually disabled by default, anyone nearby who has a WLAN adapter can see the data you broadcast. Worse still, if you don't enable secure authentication, he can connect to your network and use it as though he were wired into it. Nor is this a merely theoretical danger. Wardriving—cruising around looking for unsecured access points—has been a popular pastime since 802.11b became popular.

Various forms of wireless encryption and authentication are available, some standard and some proprietary to certain brands of gear. At a minimum, you should enable WEP (Wired Equivalent Privacy). WEP is not secure in any real sense, but it is enough to keep honest users from accidentally connecting to your system, and will deter casual snoops. WPA (Wi-Fi Protected Access) is more secure, but slightly more complicated to set up. Moreover, you'll probably need firmware updates to your WLAN gear, if not brand-spanking new gear, to use it. Read the manual for your WLAN gear and visit the maker's web site to determine what security measures are right for you and how to implement them.

What to buy

Here are the network adapters we recommend.

10/100BaseT Ethernet

If you need a wired 10/100BaseT Ethernet adapter, if possible choose a motherboard that includes an embedded PCI, CSA, or PCIe 10/100 network interface. If you need a PCI 10/100 Ethernet PCI expansion card, our first choice is the **D-Link DFE-530TX+** (*http://www.d-link.com*) and our second choice is the **Intel PRO/100 S PILA8460C3** (*http://www.intel.com*).

You want a LAN with that motherboard?

Make sure you know what you're getting when you order a motherboard. Many motherboards are available in several variants, only some of which may include embedded LAN. For example, the excellent Intel D865PERL motherboard is available in three models, one without embedded LAN (D865PERL), one with embedded 10/100 LAN (D865PERLL), and one with embedded Gigabit (1000) LAN (D865PERLK). An embedded 10/100BaseT Ethernet adapter is acceptable for most people's current needs, but Gigabit Ethernet models provide "future-proofing" at small additional cost.

10/100/1000BaseT (Gigabit) Ethernet

If you need a Gigabit-capable Ethernet adapter, if possible choose a motherboard that provides embedded Gigabit Ethernet using a CSA or PCIe interface. If you need a standalone Gigabit Ethernet adapter, our first choice is the **D-Link DGE-530T** and our second choice is the **Intel Pro/1000 MT PWLA8390MT**.

Mine, all mine

A PCI 1000 Mb/s LAN adapter can saturate the 133 MB/s PCI bus, or nearly so. Accordingly, we use PCI Gigabit LAN adapters only if there is no alternative. We prefer to use embedded Gigabit LAN that keeps LAN traffic off the PCI bus. For example, Intel motherboards with embedded Gigabit LAN route LAN traffic across the dedicated CSA (Communications Streaming Architecture) bus, leaving the PCI bus free for other purposes.

Wireless adapter

If you are building a wireless 802.11b/g network from scratch, use **D-Link DWL-G520 (PCI)**, **D-Link DWL-G122 (USB)**, and **D-Link DWL-G650 (Cardbus)** WLAN adapters. If you also need 802.11a support, use **D-Link DWL-AG530 (PCI)** and **D-Link DWL-AG660 (Cardbus)** WLAN adapters. If the WLAN adapter must interoperate with an existing wireless network, choose an 802.11g WLAN adapter made by the same company that made the existing components.

Wireless access point

If you need an 802.11b/g AP, choose the **D-Link DWL-2100AP**. If you also need 802.11a support, choose the **D-Link DWL-7100AP**.

Be a good neighbor

Configure your 802.11g network to use non-Turbo (54 Mb/s 802.11g) mode if the possibility of channel conflicts exists (e.g., if you live in an apartment or if your business is in close proximity to other businesses). Use Turbo (108 Mb/s SuperG) mode if there are no 802.11b/g APs nearby to cause conflicts. Note that you may have to replace 2.4 GHz cordless phones with models that use a different frequency band. An AP operating in Turbo mode is completely incompatible with 2.4 GHz cordless phones because it occupies nearly every channel available. An AP operating in standard 54 Mb/s 802.11g mode may or may not conflict with 2.4 GHz cordless phones. It is

supposedly possible to select specific channels for the AP and the cordless phone that allow them to operate without conflicts, although we've never had any luck doing that.

Wireless AP/Router

If you need an 802.11b/g or a/b/g AP, consider buying a model that also incorporates a hardware firewall/router. Using a hardware firewall/router on a home or SOHO network is the single most important thing you can do to improve security and reduce the likelihood that your systems will be infected by a worm. For an 802.11b/g wireless AP/router, we prefer the **D-Link DI-624**. For an 802.11a/b/g wireless AP/router, choose the **D-Link DI-784**.

Networking don'ts

Avoid HPNA adapters. If you can't run an Ethernet cable to a location that needs a network connection, use wireless Ethernet instead. Avoid no-name network adapters and other networking components. Whenever possible, avoid mixing components from different manufacturers, particularly in a wireless network.

For updated recommendations, visit *http://www.hardwareguys.com/picks/lan.html*.

Modem

A modem—a contraction of the term MOdulator/DEModulator—converts data from the digital form used by your computer to an analog form that can be transferred across an ordinary voice telephone line, and vice versa. A modem—also called a "dial-up modem" to differentiate it from cable modems and DSL modems—is typically used to connect via a POTS (Plain Old Telephone Service) line to an Internet Service Provider (ISP) or similar data service. Most current modems also support inbound and outbound faxing.

You call that a modem?

Although the terms "cable modem" and "DSL modem" are used frequently, these devices are not actually modems at all. A modem converts outbound digital data to analog and inbound analog data to digital. Cable modems and DSL modems perform no such conversion, because cable and DSL links are digital end-to-end. It is correct

to refer to Cable/DSL modems as "adapters" or "interfaces," but the incorrect usage of "modem" has become so ingrained that there is no hope of changing it.

Modems are a mature market segment. They reached their maximum possible speed—"56K," which is actually limited by law to 53K—several years ago, and modem manufacturers have since devoted few development resources to them. With few exceptions, current modems are built around one of a handful of chipsets, so the similarities between modems from different manufacturers are much greater than their differences. Most have very similar features and performance, so choosing the best model for your needs is usually a matter of deciding what type of modem you need and then balancing minor price differences against manufacturer reputations.

Use the following criteria in choosing the type of modem that is appropriate for your needs:

Transmission speed and protocols

All current modems support the so-called 56K data rate using V.90 or V.92 protocols. With perfect line and external network conditions, a V.90 modem can in theory transmit data at 31,200 bits/s and receive data at 56,000 bits/s ("56K"). In practice, regulatory limits on power levels limit the receive speed to 53,000 bits/s, and line conditions often limit it to even lower data rates. V.92 is a minor upgrade of the V.90 standard, which maintains the 53,000 bits/s receive speed of V.90, but increases transmit speed to 48,000 bits/s. Again, the theoretical data rates are seldom achieved on real-world telephone lines.

V.92 also extends the V.90 standard to add the following convenience features:

QuickConnect

Anyone who has used a dial-up modem is familiar with the series of tones that the sending and receiving modems exchange. During this "handshake" procedure, the two modems negotiate their fastest shared protocols and test the line to determine the fastest usable data rate. With V.90 modems, this handshake can require as much as 30 seconds to complete. The V.92 QuickConnect feature reduces the time necessary to establish the connection by up to 50% by storing information about modems it has previously connected to and the line conditions it experienced during earlier connections.

Modem-on-Hold

In the Bad Olde Days, if you forgot to disable call-waiting on your modem line, your data connection was unceremoniously dropped if another call came in while you were using the modem. The V.92 Modem-on-Hold feature is designed to work with call-waiting. If you are using the modem and a voice call comes in on that line, the data connection is placed on hold. You can then pick up the phone and talk to the caller. When you complete the voice call, you hang up and re-establish the data connection where you left off. Using the Modem-on-Hold feature requires explicit support by the ISP, and many ISPs have not chosen to implement it.

V.90 versus V.92

Although a few V.90 modems remain on the market, the vast majority of currently available modems support V.92. The differences between V.90 and V.92 are so minor that many existing V.90 modems can be upgraded to V.92 via a simple firmware update.

Although V.92 modems ordinarily connect to V.90 modems without any problem, we have had reports from readers who upgraded their V.90 modems to V.92 and subsequently experienced problems connecting to their ISPs. Accordingly, before you upgrade to V.92 we suggest that you make sure you can later downgrade to V.90 if necessary.

Controller-based modems versus controllerless "modems"

A true modem contains a CPU that processes outbound data before delivering it to the telephone line interface, and processes inbound data from the telephone interface before delivering it to the computer. The constant demand for lower component prices led several years ago to the introduction of so-called controllerless modems, which are also referred to as soft modems, software modems, or Winmodems. These devices are not true modems at all. They are simply hardware interfaces between the computer and the telephone line. A soft modem has no internal CPU. Instead, it uses the main system CPU to do all processing. The only advantage of a soft modem is low cost. The disadvantages are that a soft modem consumes CPU power, which may cause degraded performance; that a soft modem can be used only with an operating system that supports it, which typically means only recent versions of Windows; and that soft modems frequently drop connections and crash the computer. Don't even consider using a soft modem, regardless of how little it costs.

Internal versus external

Modems are available in internal and external versions. External modems cost a bit more than comparable internal modems because they require a case and power supply, but it's usually worth spending those few extra dollars for the additional flexibility an external modem provides.

Most internal modems are installed in a PCI expansion slot. A few are designed to fit the dedicated AMR (audio/modem riser) or CNR (communications and networking riser) slot present on some motherboards. Internal modems may be controller-based or controllerless.

External modems connect to either a serial port or a USB port. All external modems are controller-based. External modems provide status lights, which can be invaluable when you are troubleshooting connection problems. Also, external modems can be power-cycled independently of the PC if they lock up, which at times can keep you from losing all of the unsaved data in files that are open when the modem shoots craps.

Cellular modems

Cellular modems can be found in most current cellular phones as well as in dedicated cellular data cards. As with DSL and cable "modems," these are not modems at all. Well, actually they are—some cellular phones and data cards can also dial up standard modems and send or receive faxes—but this is not how most people use them. Instead, cellular modems are usually used to make a *packet data* connection to the cell tower at speeds from 40 kbps on the low end to 230 kbps and higher. The connection software you get from your cellular provider takes care of making this connection.

The advantage of cellular data is that you can get online practically anywhere you can get a signal. The downside is that you might go broke doing it: most providers bill you by the kilobyte by default. If you plan to use your phone to get online a lot, sign up for an unlimited plan. Pricing varies by provider; you'll pay anywhere from $20 to $80 a month.

It's worth taking few moments to discuss fax support. Nearly all current modems also function as fax modems, which can send faxes to and receive faxes from other fax modems and standard fax machines. When you use a fax modem, you can automatically store received faxes to your hard drive, rather than printing every fax you receive. You can then view and manage the fax data files and print only those you want in hardcopy. You can send faxes directly from word processors and other applications, and if you have a scanner you can use it to scan and fax paper documents.

Fax standards have remained relatively unchanged for more than a decade. Even the fastest dial-up modems still communicate in fax mode at only 14,400 bits/second, which was state of the art for data communications in 1991. Any modem you are likely to buy will almost certainly provide all of the fax functionality you need, if indeed you need faxing capability at all.

Why fax when you can email?

We confess that we haven't used a fax modem or a standard fax machine in years. The ubiquity of scanners and high-speed Internet connections has made faxing obsolete as far as we're concerned. When we want to "fax" something, we simply scan it and email the image file. When someone wants to fax something to us, we suggest they do the same. The image files are crisper, cleaner, and easier to use than any faxed document, particularly if you scan them at the 600 dpi used by most laser printers.

If you do need a fax and you want to share a phone line among voice, data, and fax it's worth getting multiple ring-cadence service on your phone line, which phone companies market as "RingMaster," "Distinctive Ring," or a similar name. For a small monthly charge, the phone company will associate a second telephone number with your single physical telephone line.

The ring cadence associated with each telephone number is distinctive, so when the phone rings you always know which number is being called. If someone calls the original number, which you continue using as your voice number, you hear the usual ring cadence, and answer the phone. If someone calls the second number, which is your fax number, the ring cadence is different, and you let the fax modem answer the call and receive the fax.

There are two ways to accomplish this. Some fax modems have built-in ring-cadence detectors, and can be programmed to answer only calls placed to the second number. In our experience, distinctive ring detectors built into fax modems don't always work very well. They may answer non-fax calls, or fail to answer fax calls.

The alternative is to install a standalone distinctive-ring detector, such as one of those made by Command Communications. Connect the distinctive-ring detector box at the service entrance, with the first output connected straight through to your telephone wiring. (Most distinctive-ring detector boxes produce sufficient ring current on each output to ring several phones.) Connect the second output directly to the fax modem. This method eliminates ambiguity. Your telephones receive a ring signal only for calls that are placed to the voice number, and therefore ring only when you receive a voice call. Your fax modem receives a ring signal only for calls placed to the fax number, which it can answer silently.

If you use this method, it's a good idea to install blocking devices on each of your voice telephones to prevent you from picking up the phone while a fax call is in progress. These blocking devices sell for a few dollars and are available at any telephone store, usually described as an "answering machine blocker" or something similar. They plug into a standard telephone jack and have two output jacks, one labeled "Tel" and one labeled "Ans". If a phone connected to a "Tel" jack is picked up, it disconnects any off-hook device connected to an "Ans" jack. Conversely, if a "Tel" device is off-hook and you pick up a telephone connected to an "Ans" jack, you hear only dead air. Connect the fax modem to the "Tel" jack to prevent it from being interrupted, and connect each of your voice telephones to the "Ans" jack so that they can seize control of the line only if the fax modem is not using it.

What to buy

Here are the modems we recommend.

External modem
: For general use, buy an external V.90 or V.92 controller-based modem. If you want the best modem available, bar none, buy the **U.S. Robotics Courier 56K V.92 Business Modem**, (*http://www.usrobotics.com*), which can establish and maintain connections under line conditions so bad that other modems don't even attempt to connect. For a less expensive but still excellent external modem, buy the **U.S. Robotics USR5633A 56K USB Fax modem.**

Internal modem
: If for some reason you must have an internal modem, choose the **U.S. Robotics USR5699B 56K V.92 Internal Fax modem PCI.**

Modem don'ts

We recommend you avoid internal modems in general, whether they are controller-based or controllerless. In particular, avoid controllerless "soft modems" if you run Linux. Avoid no-name modems of any description.

For updated recommendations, visit *http://www.hardwareguys.com/picks/modem.html.*

2
Buying Components

We've bought hundreds of thousands of dollars' worth of PC components over the last 20 years, for ourselves and on behalf of employers and clients. In the following sections, we'll tell you what we learned along the way.

Buying Guidelines

Until the early 1990s, most computer products were bought in computer specialty stores. Retail sales still make up a significant chunk of computer product sales—although the emphasis has shifted from computer specialty stores to local "big box" retailers like Best Buy, CompUSA, Wal-Mart, and Costco—but online resellers now account for a large percentage of PC component sales.

Should you buy from a local brick-and-mortar retailer or an online reseller? We do both, because each has advantages and disadvantages.

Local retailers offer the inestimable advantage of instant gratification. Unless you're more patient than we are, when you want something, you want it *right now*. Buying from a local retailer puts the product in your hands instantly, instead of making you wait for FedEx to show up. You can also hold the product in your hands, something that's not possible if you buy from an online reseller. Local retailers also have a big advantage if you need to return or exchange a product. If something doesn't work right, or if you simply change your mind, you can just drive back to the store rather than dealing with the hassles and cost of returning a product to an online reseller.

Online resellers have the advantage in breadth and depth of product selection. If you want the less-expensive OEM version of a product, for example, chances are you won't find it at local retailer's, most of which stock only retail-boxed products. If an online reseller stocks a particular manufacturer's products, it tends to stock the entire product line, whereas local retailers often pick and choose only the most popular items in a product line. (Of course, the popular products are usually popular for good reasons.) Online resellers are also more likely to stock niche products and products from smaller manufacturers. Sometimes, if you must have a particular product, the only option is to buy it online.

Online resellers usually advertise lower prices than local retailers, but it's a mistake to compare only nominal prices. When you buy from a local retailer, you pay only the advertised price plus any applicable sales tax. When you buy from an online retailer, you pay the advertised price plus shipping, which may end up costing you more than buying locally.

No sales tax? Think again

Ah, but you don't have to pay sales tax when you buy online, right? Well, maybe. In most jurisdictions, you're required by law to pay a *use tax* in lieu of sales tax on out-of-state purchases. Most people evade use taxes, of course, but that free ride is coming to an end. States faced with increasing budget problems, which is to say all of them, are starting to clamp down on people who buy from online resellers and don't pay use tax. States are using data-mining techniques to coordinate with each other and with credit card companies and online retailers to uncover unpaid use taxes. If you don't pay use taxes, one day soon you're likely to hear from the audit division of your state department of revenue, asking what these credit card charges were for and why you didn't report the use taxes due on them. Count on it.

Although online resellers *may* have a lower overall price on a given component, it's a mistake to assume that this is always the case. Local retailers frequently run sales and rebate promotions that cut the price of a component below the lowest online price. For example, we bought a spindle of 100 CD-R discs on sale from a local retailer for $19.95 with a $10 instant rebate and a $20 mail-in rebate. After the cost of the stamp to mail in the rebate form, they *paid* us $9.68 to carry away those 100 discs, which is pretty tough for an online reseller to match. Similarly, we bought an 80 GB hard drive for $79.95, with a $15 instant rebate and a $30 mail-in rebate. Net cost? About $35 for a retail-boxed 80 GB hard drive, which no online vendor could come close to matching.

In particular, local retailers are usually the best place to buy heavy and/or bulky items, such as monitors, cases, UPSs, and so on. Local retailers receive these items in pallet loads, which makes the cost of shipping an individual item almost nothing. Conversely, online resellers have to charge you, directly or indirectly, for the cost of getting that heavy item to your door.

Whether you purchase your PC components from a local brick-and-mortar store or a web-based retailer, here are some guidelines to keep in mind:

- Make sure you know exactly what you're buying. For example, a hard drive may be available in two versions, each with the same or a similar model number but with an added letter or number to designate different amounts of cache. Or a hard drive maker may produce two models of the same size that differ in price and performance. Always compare using the exact manufacturer model number. Before you buy a product, research it on the manufacturer's web site and on the numerous independent web sites devoted to reviews. We usually search Google with the product name and "review" in the search string.
- Vendors vary greatly. Some we trust implicitly, and others we wouldn't order from on a bet. Some are always reliable, others always unreliable, and still others seem to vary with the phases of the moon. We check *http://www.resellerratings.com*, which maintains a database of customer-reported experiences with hundreds of vendors.
- The list price or Suggested Retail Price (SRP) is meaningless. Most computer products sell for a fraction of SRP, others sell for near SRP, and for still others the manufacturer has no SRP, but instead publishes an Estimated Selling Price (ESP). To do meaningful comparisons, you need to know what different vendors charge for the product. Fortunately, there are many services that list what various vendors charge. We use *http://www.pricescan.com*, *http://www.pricewatch.com*, and *http://www.pricegrabber.com*. These services may list 20 or more different vendors, and the prices for a particular item may vary dramatically. We discard the top 25% and the bottom 25% and eyeball-average the middle 50% to decide a reasonable price for the item.

Have we got a deal for you...

If you like getting good deals (and who doesn't?), check out sites dealnews (*http://www.dealnews.com*) and SlickDeals (*http://www.slickdeals.net*), which are great for finding rebates and sales.

- Many components are sold in retail-boxed and OEM forms. The core component is likely to be similar or identical in either case, but important details may vary. For example, Intel CPUs are available in retail-boxed versions that include a CPU cooler and a three-year warranty. They are also available as OEM components (also called *tray packaging* or *white box*) that do not include the CPU cooler and have only a 90-day warranty. OEM items are not intended for retail distribution, so some manufacturers provide no warranty to individual purchasers. OEM components are fine, as long as you understand the differences and do not attempt to compare prices between retail-boxed and OEM.

- The market for PCs and components is incredibly competitive and margins are razor-thin. If a vendor advertises a component for much less than other vendors, it may be a "loss leader." More likely, though, particularly if its prices on other items are similarly low, that vendor cuts corners, whether by using your money to float inventory, by shipping returned product as new, by charging excessive shipping fees, or, in the ultimate case, by taking your money and not shipping the product. If you always buy from the vendor with the rock-bottom price, you'll waste a lot of time hassling with returns of defective, used, or discontinued items and dealing with your credit card company when the vendor fails to deliver at all. Ultimately, you're also likely to spend more money than you would have by buying from a reputable vendor in the first place.
- The actual price you pay may vary significantly from the advertised price. When you compare prices, include all charges, particularly shipping charges. Reputable vendors tell you exactly how much the total charges will be. Less reputable vendors may forget to mention shipping charges, which may be very high. Some vendors break out the full manufacturer pack into individual items. For example, if a retail-boxed hard drive includes mounting hardware, some vendors will quote a price for the bare drive without making it clear that they have removed the mounting hardware and charge separately for it. Also be careful when buying products that include a rebate from the maker. Some vendors quote the net price after rebate without making it clear that they are doing so.
- Some vendors charge more for an item ordered via their 800 number than they do for the same item ordered directly from their web site. Some others add a fixed processing fee to phone orders. These charges reflect the fact that taking orders on the web is much cheaper than doing it by phone, so this practice has become common. In fact, some of our favorite vendors, such as NewEgg.com, do not provide telephone order lines.
- It can be very expensive to ship heavy items such as CRTs, UPSs, and printers individually. This is one situation in which local big-box stores like Best Buy have a huge advantage over online vendors. The online vendor has to charge you for the cost of shipping, directly or indirectly, and that cost can amount to $50 or more for a heavy item that you need quickly. Conversely, the big-box stores receive inventory items in

truckload or even railcar shipments, so the cost to them to have a single item delivered is quite small. They can pass that reduced cost on to buyers. If you're buying a heavy item, don't assume that it will be cheaper online. Check your local Best Buy or other big-box store and you may find that it actually costs less there, even after you pay sales tax. And you can carry it away with you instead of waiting for FedEx to show up with it.

- Most direct resellers are willing to sell for less than the price they advertise. All you need do is tell your chosen vendor that you'd really rather buy from them, but not at the price they're quoting. Use lower prices you find with the price comparison services as a wedge to get a better price. But remember that reputable vendors must charge more than the fly-by-night operations if they are to make a profit and stay in business. If we're ordering by phone, we generally try to beat down our chosen vendor a bit on price, but we don't expect them to match the rock-bottom prices that turn up on web searches. Of course, if you're ordering from a web-only vendor, dickering is not an option, which is one reason why web-only vendors generally have better prices.
- Using a credit card puts the credit card company on your side if there is a problem with your order. If the vendor ships the wrong product, a defective product, or no product at all, you can invoke charge-back procedures to have the credit card company refund your money. Vendors who live and die on credit card orders cannot afford to annoy credit card companies, and so tend to resolve such problems quickly. Even your threat to request a charge-back may cause a recalcitrant vendor to see reason.
- Some vendors add a surcharge, typically 3%, to their advertised prices if you pay by credit card. Surcharges violate credit card company contracts, so some vendors instead offer a similar discount for paying cash, which amounts to the same thing. Processing credit card transactions costs money, and we're sure that some such vendors are quite reputable, but our own experience with vendors that surcharge has not been good. We always suspect that their business practices result in a high percentage of charge-back requests, and so they discourage using credit cards.
- Good vendors allow you to return a defective product for replacement or a full refund (often less shipping charges) within a stated period, typically 30 days. Buy only from such vendors. Nearly all vendors exclude some product categories, such as notebook computers, monitors, printers, and opened software, either because their contracts with the manufacturer require them to do so or because some buyers

commonly abuse return periods for these items, treating them as "30-day free rentals." Beware of the phrase, "All sales are final." That means exactly what it says.

A cunning plan

Nearly all retailers refuse to refund your money on opened software, DVDs, etc., but will only exchange the open product for a new, sealed copy of the same title. One of our readers tells us how he gets around that common policy. He returns the open software in exchange for a new, sealed copy of the same product, keeping his original receipt. He then returns the new, sealed copy for a refund. That's probably unethical and may be illegal for all we know, but it does work.

- Check carefully for any mention of restocking fees. Many vendors who trumpet a "no questions asked money-back guarantee" mention only in the fine print that they won't refund all your money. They charge a restocking fee on returns, and we've seen fees as high as 30% of the purchase price. These vendors love returns, because they make a lot more money if you return the product than if you keep it. Do not buy from a vendor that charges restocking fees on exchanges (as opposed to refunds). For refunds, accept no restocking fee higher than 10% to 15%, depending on the price of the item.

The customer isn't always right

Even some of our favorite vendors have started charging restocking fees in response to abuses by customers (see the previous Note). Yes, there are sleazy customers as well as sleazy resellers. For example, we heard from one guy who was desperate to get his hands on the latest high-end video adapter as soon as possible. No reseller had the video card in stock yet, and everyone had a waiting list. This sweetheart ordered the same card from three or four different resellers, hoping to maximize his chances of getting it quickly.

He installed the first one that arrived, and returned the others, claiming they were defective. He demanded a full refund, including shipping both ways! He even opened the boxes to "prove" he'd attempted to use them. If he'd asked for replacements, there wouldn't have been any problem, but he wanted a refund. Naturally, the victimized resellers refused to refund the shipping costs and charged him a restocking fee. He was outraged, and emailed me to

suggest I warn my readers not to buy from those resellers. He seemed surprised that I had no sympathy for him. Nowadays, he'd probably auction the extra ones on eBay and make a killing.

Most of the better resellers that charge restocking fees do so to protect themselves against such abuses, and most are willing to make exceptions on a case-by-case basis. Before you buy from a reseller, verify its restocking fees and policies and determine under what conditions they are willing to make exceptions.

- If you order by phone, don't accept verbal promises. Insist that the reseller confirm your order in writing, including any special terms or conditions, before charging your credit card or shipping product. If a reseller balks at providing written confirmation of their policies, terms, and conditions, find another vendor. Most are happy to do so. If you're ordering from a vendor that uses web-based ordering exclusively, use a screen capture program or your browser's save function to grab copies of each screen as you complete the order. Most vendors send a confirming email, which we file in our "Never Delete" folder.
- File everything related to an order, including a copy of the original advertisement, email, faxed or written confirmations provided by the reseller, copies of your credit card receipt, a copy of the packing list and invoice, and so on. We also jot down notes in our PIM regarding telephone conversations, including the date, time, telephone number and extension, person spoken to, purpose of the call, and so on. We print a copy of those to add to the folder for that order.
- Make it clear to the reseller that you expect them to ship the exact item you have ordered, not what they consider to be an "equivalent substitute." Require that they confirm the exact items they will ship, including manufacturer part numbers. For example, if you order an ATi RADEON X800 XT Platinum Edition PCIe graphics card, make sure the order confirmation specifies that item by name, full description, and ATi product number. Don't accept a less detailed description such as "graphics card," "ATi graphics card," or even "ATi RADEON X800 graphics card." Otherwise, you almost certainly won't get what you paid for. You may get an X800 Pro AGP model rather than the X800 XT Platinum Edition PCIe model you ordered, a plain X800 XT rather than the more expensive X800 XT Platinum Edition, an OEM card with a slower processor or less memory, or even a "Powered by ATi" card—which is to say a card with an ATi processor made by another manufacturer—rather than a "Built by ATi" card. Count on it.

- Verify warranty terms. Some manufacturers warrant only items purchased from authorized dealers in full retail packaging. For some items, the warranty begins when the manufacturer ships the product to the distributor, which may be long before you receive it. OEM products typically have much shorter warranties than retail-boxed products—sometimes as short as 90 days—and may be warranted only to the original distributor rather than to the final buyer. Better resellers may *endorse the manufacturer warranty* for some period on some products, often 30 to 90 days. That means that if the product fails, you can return the item to the reseller, who will ship you a replacement and take care of dealing with the manufacturer. Some resellers disclaim the manufacturer warranty, claiming that once they ship the item dealing with warranty claims is your problem, even if the product arrives DOA. We've encountered that problem a couple of times. Usually, mentioning phrases like *merchantability and fitness for a particular purpose* and *revocation of acceptance* leads them to see reason quickly. We usually demand the reseller ship us a new replacement product immediately and include a prepaid return shipping label if they want the dead item back. We don't accept or pay for dead merchandise under any circumstances, and neither should you.
- Direct resellers are required by law to ship products within the time period they promise. But that time period may be precise (e.g., "ships within 24 hours") or vague (e.g., "ships within three to six weeks"). If the vendor cannot ship by the originally promised date, it must notify you in writing and specify another date by which the item will ship. If that occurs, you have the right to cancel your order without penalty. Make sure to make clear to the reseller that you expect the item to be delivered in a timely manner. Reputable vendors ship what they say they're going to ship when they say they're going to ship it. Unfortunately, some vendors have a nasty habit of taking your money and shipping whenever they get around to it. In a practice that borders on fraud, some vendors routinely report items as "in stock" when in fact they are not. Make it clear to the vendor that you do not authorize them to charge your credit card until the item actually ships, and that if you do not receive the item when promised you will cancel the order.

Even if you follow all of these guidelines, you may have a problem. Even the best resellers sometimes drop the ball. If that happens, don't expect the problem to go away by itself. If you encounter a problem, remain calm and notify the reseller first. Good resellers are anxious to resolve problems. Find out how the reseller wants to proceed, and follow their procedures, particularly for labeling returned merchandise with an RMA number. If things seem not be going as they should, explain to the vendor why you are dissatisfied, and tell them that you plan to request a charge-back from your credit card company. Finally, if the reseller is entirely recalcitrant and any aspect of the transaction (including, for example, a confirmation letter you wrote) took place via U.S. Postal Service, contact your postmaster about filing charges of mail fraud. That really gets a reseller's attention, but use it as a last resort.

Recommended Sources

The question we hear more often than any other is, "What company should I buy from?" When someone asks us that question, we run away, screaming in terror. Well, not really, but we'd like to. Answering that question is a no-win proposition for us, you see. If we recommend a vendor and that vendor treats the buyer properly, well that's no more than was expected. But Thor forbid that we recommend a vendor who turns around and screws the buyer.

Robert the Red

Yes, it's true. Robert is of Viking extraction. On government forms, he describes himself as "Viking-American." And, no, he doesn't wear a funny helmet. Except among friends. And he hasn't pillaged anything in months. Years, maybe.

So, which online resellers do we buy from? Over the years, we've bought from scores of online vendors, and our favorites have changed. For the last few years, our favorite has been NewEgg (*http://www.newegg.com*). NewEgg offers an extraordinarily good combination of price, wide product selection, support, shipping, and return or replacement policies. We know of no other direct vendor that even comes close.

NewEgg's prices aren't always rock-bottom, but they generally match any other vendor we're willing to deal with. NewEgg runs daily specials that are often real bargains, so if you're willing to consider alternatives and to accumulate components over the course of a few weeks you can save a fair amount of money. (Of course, if you do that, your warranty and return privileges on earlier orders are winding down as you wait.) NewEgg ships what they say they're going to ship, when they say they're going to ship it, and at the price they agreed to ship it for. If there's a problem, they make it right. It's hard to do better than that.

Piscatory Mortality

All of that said, if you buy from NewEgg and subsequently your goldfish dies and all of your teeth fall out, don't blame us. All we can say is that NewEgg has always treated us right. Things can change overnight in this industry and, while we don't expect NewEgg to take a sudden turn for the worse, it could happen.

As to local retailers, we buy from—in no particular order—Best Buy, CompUSA, Target, Office Depot, OfficeMax, and our local computer specialty stores, depending on what we need and who happens to have advertised the best prices and rebates in the Sunday ad supplements. Wal-Mart used to sell only assembled PCs. It has recently started stocking PC components, such as ATi video adapters, so we'll add Wal-Mart to our list as well.

Yet another cunning plan...

If you buy from a local retailer, open the box from the bottom rather than the top. If you need to return a non-defective item, that makes it easier to repackage the product with the manufacturer's seals intact, which can help avoid restocking fees.

Index

C

D

E

F

G

H

I

J

K

L

M

Q

R

S

T

U

V

W

Z

About the Authors

Robert Bruce Thompson is the author or coauthor of numerous online training courses and computer books. Robert built his first computer in 1976 from discrete chips. It had 256 *bytes* of memory, used toggle switches and LEDs for I/O, ran at less than 1 MHz, and had no operating system. Since then, he has bought, built, upgraded, and repaired hundreds of PCs for himself, employers, customers, friends, and clients. Robert reads mysteries and nonfiction for relaxation, but only on cloudy nights. He spends most clear, moonless nights outdoors with his 10" Dobsonian reflector telescope, hunting down faint fuzzies, and is currently designing a larger truss-tube Dobsonian (computerized, of course) that he plans to build.

Barbara Fritchman Thompson worked for twenty years as a librarian before starting her own home-based consulting practice, Research Solutions *(http://www.researchsolutions.net)*, and is also a researcher for the law firm Womble Carlyle Sandridge & Rice, PLLC. Barbara, who has been a PC power user for more than 15 years, researched and tested much of the hardware reviewed for this book. During her leisure hours, Barbara reads, works out, plays golf, and, like Robert, is an avid amateur astronomer.

Colophon

Our look is the result of reader comments, our own experimentation, and feedback from distribution channels. Distinctive covers complement our distinctive approach to technical topics, breathing personality and life into potentially dry subjects.

Darren Kelly was the production editor and Sada Preisch was the proofreader for *PC Hardware Buyer's Guide*. Marcia Friedman did the typesetting and page makeup. Claire Cloutier provided quality control. Reg Aubry wrote the index.

Marcia Friedman designed the cover of this book using Adobe InDesign CS. Emma Colby produced the cover layout with Adobe InDesign CS using Berthold Akzindenz Grotesk and Adobe's Trade Gothic fonts. Emma Colby designed the reference card with Adobe InDesign CS using Adobe's Carta, ITC Zapf Dingbats, Sabon, Trade Gothic, and Monotype Transport fonts.

Marcia Friedman designed and implemented the interior layout using Adobe InDesign CS. The text and heading fonts are Sabon, Trade Gothic, and Berthold Akzidenz Grotesk. The illustrations and screenshots that appear in the book were produced by Robert Romano and Jessamyn Read using Macromedia FreeHand MX and Adobe Photoshop 7.